# The Poetry of Samuel Rogers

## Including; The Pleasures of Memory

Samuel Rogers was born on 30th July 1763 at Newington Green, at the time a village north of Islington, London and was educated in Hackney and Stoke Newington.

Although Rogers wished to enter the Presbyterian ministry, his father persuaded him to join the family banking business in Cornhill. He complied with his fathers' wishes but his frail health provided an excuse to take time off from work and much of this time was spent on a steadily growing interest in English literature, particularly the works of Samuel Johnson, Thomas Gray and Oliver Goldsmith.

His circumstances now allowed him to try writing poetry himself. He began with contributions to the Gentleman's Magazine, and in 1786 he published a volume containing some imitations of Goldsmith and an "Ode to Superstition" in the style of Gray.

In 1788 his elder brother sadly Thomas died, and Rogers was called upon to increase his responsibilities to the family business.

However, Rogers still set aside time to work on his poetry. Using Gray as his model (who was exceedingly slow at producing finished poems), Rogers spent much time polishing his verses, and it was six years after the publication of his first volume before he published his next: The Pleasures of Memory in 1792.

In 1793 his father died and Rogers now inherited the principal share of the banking house in Cornhill, and attached to it was a considerable income.

Rogers could now use both his business influence, power and money with that of his literary career and conversational ability to be at the very centre of literary and social London. It was a role in which he was masterful.

At the time social breakfasts were very popular in London. Rogers was a noted host of these and many clamoured for his attention, eye and an invitation. His dinner parties were open to only a very select few. His powers as a conversationalist, his educated taste in all matters of art, and his sarcastic and bitter wit, for which he excused himself by saying that he had such a small voice that no one listened if he said pleasant things, combined to make him perhaps London's most powerful host.

"He certainly had the kindest heart and unkindest tongue of any one I ever knew," said Fanny Kemble. He helped the Francis Jeffrey reconcile with Byron, and he relieved Sheridan's difficulties in the last days of his life. The Irish poet, Thomas Moore, who refused help from everyone, and would only owe debts to his publishers, found it possible to accept help from Rogers. He also procured a pension for HF Cary, the translator of Dante, and obtained for Wordsworth his sinecure as distributor of stamps.

Rogers made his poetic reputation with The Pleasures of Memory when William Cowper's fame was still in the making. As well as friendships with Wordsworth, Walter Scott and Byron, he was asked for, on the death of Wordsworth, and after declining the post for himself, his opinion on the fitness of Alfred Tennyson for the post of Poet Laureate.

Rogers was held in high esteem by many other institutions. He was a trustee of the National Gallery; and he served on a commission regarding the management of the British Museum, and yet another for the rebuilding of the Houses of Parliament. In November 1796 he was elected a Fellow of the Royal Society.

His writing output though remained almost painfully slow. An Epistle to a Friend, published in 1798, describes his ideal of a happy life. This was followed by The Voyage of Columbus (1810), and by Jacqueline (1814), a narrative poem, written in the four-accent measure of the newer writers, and published in the same volume with Byron's Lara. His reflective poem on Human Life (1819), on which he had worked on for twelve years, is written in his earlier manner.

In 1814 Rogers toured the Continent with his sister Sarah. They travelled through Switzerland to Italy, keeping a full diary of events and impressions as they went. At Naples the news of Napoleon's escape from Elba ensured a return home to England.

Seven years later he returned to Italy and visited Byron and Shelley in Pisa. From his experiences on these tours came his last and longest work, Italy. The first part was published in 1822 and the second followed in 1828. At first it failed to gain an audience but Rogers was determined to make it successful. He first enlarged and revised the poem, and then commissioned illustrations from J.M.W. Turner, Thomas Stothard and Samuel Prout. These were engraved on steel in the sumptuous edition of 1830. The revised edition was a great success. Rogers then followed the same treatment with an equally sumptuous edition of his Poems in 1834.

For the last five years of his life he was confined to his chair in consequence of a fall in the street. He died in London at age 92 on 18th December 1855, and is buried in the family tomb in the churchyard of St Mary's Church, Hornsey High Street, Haringey.

## Index of Contents

## THE PLEASURES OF MEMORY

Oh could my Mind, unfolded in my page,
Enlighten climes and mould a future age;
There as it glow'd, with noblest frenzy fraught,
Dispense the treasures of exalted thought;
To Virtue wake the pulses of the heart,
And bid the tear of emulation start!
Oh could it still, thro' each succeeding year,
My life, my manners, and my name endear;
And, when the poet sleeps in silent dust,
Still hold communion with the wise and just!
Yet should this Verse, my leisure's best resource,
When thro' the world it steals its secret course,
Revive but once a generous wish supprest,
Chase but a sigh, or charm a care to rest;
In one good deed a fleeting hour employ,
Or flush one faded cheek with honest joy;
Blest were my lines, tho' limited their sphere,
Tho' short their date, as his who trac'd them here.

## PART I

*Dolce sentier.......*
*Colle, che mi piacesti,....*
*Ov' ancor per usanza Amor mi mena;*
*Ben riconosco in voi l'usate forme,*
*Non, lasso, in me.*
*PETRARCH*

## ANALYSIS OF THE FIRST PART

The Poem begins with the description of an obscure village, and of the pleasing melancholy which it excites on being revisited after a long absence. This mixed sensation is an effect of the Memory.

From an effect we naturally ascend to the cause; and the subject proposed is then unfolded with an investigation of the nature and leading principles of this faculty.

It is evident that our ideas flow in continual succession, and introduce each other with a certain degree of regularity.

They are sometimes excited by sensible objects, and sometimes by an internal operation of the mind. Of the former species is most probably the memory of brutes; and its many sources of pleasure to them, as well as to us, are considered in the first part. The latter is the most perfect degree of memory, and forms the subject of the second.

When ideas have any relation whatever, they are attractive of each other in the mind; and the perception of any object naturally leads to the idea of another, which was connected with it either in time or place, or which can be compared or contrasted with it. Hence arises our attachment to inanimate objects; hence also, in some degree, the love of our country, and the emotion with which we contemplate the celebrated scenes of antiquity. Hence a picture directs our thoughts to the original: and, as cold and darkness suggest forcibly the ideas of heat and light, he, who feels the infirmities of age, dwells most on wh atever reminds him of the vigour and vivacity of his youth.

The associating principle, as here employed, is no less conducive to virtue than to happiness; and, as such, it frequently discovers itself in the most tumultuous scenes of life. It addresses our finer feelings, and gives exercise to every mild and generous propensity.

Not confined to man, it extends through all animated nature; and its effects are peculiarly striking in the domestic tribes.


Twilight's soft dews steal o'er the village-green,
With magic tints to harmonize the scene.
Still'd is the hum that thro' the hamlet broke,
When round the ruins of their antient oak
The peasants flock'd to hear the minstrel play,
And games and carols clos'd the busy day.
Her wheel at rest, the matron thrills no more
With treasur'd tales, and legendary lore.
All, all are fled; nor mirth nor music flows
To chase the dreams of innocent repose.
All, all are fled; yet still I linger here!
What secret charms this silent spot endear?
Mark yon old Mansion frowning thro' the trees.
Whose hollow turret wooes the whistling breeze.
That casement, arch'd with ivy's brownest shade,
First to these eyes the light of heav'n convey'd.
The mouldering gateway strews the grass-grown court,
Once the calm scene of many a simple sport;
When nature pleas'd, for life itself was new,
And the heart promis'd what the fancy drew.
See, thro' the fractur'd pediment reveal'd,
Where moss inlays the rudely-sculptur'd shield,
The martin's old, hereditary nest.

Long may the ruin spare its hallow'd guest!
As jars the hinge, what sullen echoes call!
Oh haste, unfold the hospitable hall!
That hall, where once, in antiquated state,
The chair of justice held the grave debate.
Now stain'd with dews, with cobwebs darkly hung,
Oft has its roof with peals of rapture rung;
When round yon ample board, in due degree,
We sweeten'd every meal with social glee.
The heart's light laugh pursued the circling jest;
And all was sunshine in each little breast.
'Twas here we chas'd the slipper by the sound;
And turn'd the blindfold hero round and round.
'Twas here, at eve, we form'd our fairy ring;
And Fancy flutter'd on her wildest wing.
Giants and genii chain'd each wondering ear;
And orphan-sorrows drew the ready tear.
Oft with the babes we wander'd in the wood,
Or view'd the forest-feats of Robin Hood:
Oft, fancy-led, at midnight's fearful hour,
With startling step we seal'd the lonely tower:
O'er infant innocence to hang and weep,
Murder'd by ruffian hands, when smiling in its sleep.
Ye Household Deities! whose guardian eye
Mark'd each pure thought, ere register'd on high;
Still, still ye walk the consecrated ground,
And breathe the soul of Inspiration round.
As o'er the dusky furniture I bend,
Each chair awakes the feelings of a friend.
The storied arras, source of fond delight,
With old achievement charms the wilder'd sight;
And still, with Heraldry's rich hues imprest,
On the dim window glows the pictur'd crest.
The screen unfolds its many-colour'd chart.
The clock still points its moral to the heart.
That faithful monitor 'twas heav'n to hear!
When soft it spoke a promis'd pleasure near:
And has its sober hand, its simple chime,
Forgot to trace the feather'd feet of Time?
That massive beam, with curious carvings wrought,
Whence the caged linnet sooth'd my pensive thought;
Those muskets, cas'd with venerable rust;
Those once-lov'd forms, still breathing thro' their dust,
Still from the frame, in mould gigantic cast,
Starting to life all whisper of the past!
As thro' the garden's desert paths I rove,
What fond illusions swarm in every grove!
How oft, when purple evening ting'd the west,
We watch'd the emmet to her grainy nest;
Welcom'd the wild-bee home on weary wing,
Laden with sweets, the choicest of the spring!

How oft inscrib'd, with 'Friendship's votive rhyme,
The bark now silver'd by the touch of Time;
Soar'd in the swing, half pleas'd and half afraid,
Thro' sister elms that wav'd their summer-shade;
Or strew'd with crumbs yon root-inwoven seat,
To lure the redbreast from his lone retreat!
Childhood's lov'd group revisits every scene;
The tangled wood-walk, and the tufted green!
Indulgent MEMORY wakes, and lo, they live!
Cloth'd with far softer hues than Light can give.
Thou first, best friend that Heav'n assigns below,
To sooth and sweeten all the cares we know;
Whose glad suggestions still each vain alarm,
When nature fades, and life forgets to charm;
Thee would the Muse invoke! to thee belong
The sage's precept, and the poet's song.
What soften'd views thy magic glass reveals,
When o'er the landscape Time's meek twilight steals!
As when in ocean sinks the orb of day,
Long on the wave reflected lustres play;
Thy temper'd gleams of happiness resign'd
Glance on the darken'd mirror of the mind.
The School's lone porch, with reverend mosses gray,
Just tells the pensive pilgrim where it lay.
Mute is the bell that rung at peep of dawn,
Quickening my truant-feet across the lawn:
Unheard the shout that rent the noontide air,
When the slow dial gave a pause to care.
Up springs, at every step, to claim a tear,
Some little friendship form'd and cherish'd here!
And not the lightest leaf, but trembling teems
With golden visions, and romantic dreams!
Down by yon hazel copse, at evening, blaz'd
The Gipsy's faggot, there we stood and gaz'd;
Gaz'd on her sun-burnt face with silent awe,
Her tatter'd mantle, and her hood of straw;
Her moving lips, her caldron brimming o'er;
The drowsy brood that on her back she bore,
Imps, in the barn with mousing owlet bred,
From rifled roost at nightly revel fed;
Whose dark eyes flash'd thro' locks of blackest shade,
When in the breeze the distant watch-dog bay'd:
And heroes fled the Sibyl's mutter'd call,
Whose elfin prowess scal'd the orchard-wall.
As o'er my palm the silver piece she drew,
And trac'd the line of life with searching view,
How throbb'd my fluttering pulse with hopes and fears,
To learn the colour of my future years!
Ah, then, what honest triumph flush'd my breast!
This truth once known. To bless is to be blest!
We led the bending beggar on his way,

(Bare were his feet, his tresses silver-gray)
Sooth'd the keen pangs his aged spirit felt,
And on his tale with mute attention dwelt.
As in his scrip we dropt our little store,
And wept to think that little was no more,
He breath'd his prayer, "Long may such goodness live!"
'Twas all he gave, 'twas all he had to give.
Angels, when Mercy's mandate wing'd their flight,
Had stopt to catch new rapture from the sight.
But hark! thro' those old firs, with sullen swell
The church-clock strikes! ye tender scenes, farewell!
It calls me hence, beneath their shade, to trace
The few fond lines that Time may soon efface.
On yon gray stone, that fronts the chancel-door.
Worn smooth by busy feet now seen no more,
Each eve we shot the marble thro' the ring,
When the heart danc'd, and life was in its spring;
Alas! unconscious of the kindred earth,
That faintly echoed to the voice of mirth.
The glow-worm loves her emerald light to shed,
Where now the sexton rests his hoary head.
Oft, as he turn'd the greensward with his spade,
He lectur'd every youth that round him play'd;
And, calmly pointing where his fathers lay,
Rous'd him to rival each, the hero of his day.
Hush, ye fond flutterings, hush! while here alone
I search the records of each mouldering stone.
Guides of my life! Instructors of my youth!
Who first unveil'd the hallow'd form of Truth;
Whose every word enlighten'd and endear'd;
In age belov'd, in poverty rever'd;
In Friendship's silent register ye live,
Nor ask the vain memorial Art can give.
But when the sons of peace and pleasure sleep,
When only Sorrow wakes, and wakes to weep,
What spells entrance my visionary mind,
With sighs so sweet, with transports so refin'd?
Ethereal Power! whose smile, at noon of night,
Recalls the far-fled spirit of delight;
Instils that musing, melancholy mood,
Which charms the wise, and elevates the good;
Blest MEMORY, hail! Oh grant the grateful Muse,
Her pencil dipt in Nature's living hues,
To pass the clouds that round thy empire roll,
And trace its airy precincts in the soul.
Lull'd in the countless chambers of the brain,
Our thoughts are link'd by many a hidden chain.
Awake but one, and lo, what myriads rise!
Each stamps its image as the other flies!
Each, as the various avenues of sense
Delight or sorrow to the soul dispense,

Brightens or fades; yet all, with magic art,
Controul the latent fibres of the heart.
As studious PROSPERO'S mysterious spell
Conven'd the subject-spirits to his cell;
Each, at thy call, advances or retires,
As judgment dictates, or the scene inspires.
Each thrills the seat of sense, that sacred source
Whence the fine nerves direct their mazy course,
And thro' the frame invisibly convey
The subtle, quick vibrations as they play.
Survey the globe, each ruder realm explore;
From Reason's faintest ray to NEWTON soar,
What different spheres to human bliss assign'd!
What slow gradations in the scale of mind!
Yet mark in each these mystic wonders wrought;
Oh mark the sleepless energies of thought!
The adventurous boy, that asks his little share,
And hies from home with many a gossip's prayer,
Turns on the neighbouring hill, once more to see
The dear abode of peace and privacy;
And as he turns, the thatch among the trees,
The smoke's blue wreaths ascending with the breeze,
The village-common spotted white with sheep,
The church-yard yews round which his fathers sleep;
All rouse Reflection's sadly-pleasing train.
And oft he looks and weeps, and looks again.
So, when the mild TUPIA dar'd explore
Arts yet untaught, and worlds unknown before,
And, with the sons of Science, woo'd the gale
That, rising, swell'd their strange expanse of sail;
So, when he breath'd his firm yet fond adieu,
Borne from his leafy hut, his carv'd canoe,
And all his soul best lov'd, such tears he shed,
While each soft scene of summer-beauty fled:
Long o'er the wave a wistful look he cast,
Long watch'd the streaming signal from the mast;
Till twilight's dewy tints deceiv'd his eye,
And fairy forests fring'd the evening sky.
So Scotia's Queen, as slowly dawn'd the day,'
Rose on her couch, and gaz'd her soul away.
Her eyes had bless'd the beacon's glimmering height,
That faintly tipt the feathery surge with light;
But now the morn with orient hues pourtray'd
Each castled cliff, and brown monastic shade:
All touch'd the talisman's resistless spring,
And lo, what busy tribes were instant on the wing!
Thus kindred objects kindred thoughts inspire,
As summer-clouds flash forth electric fire.
And hence this spot gives back the joys of youth,
Warm as the life, and with the mirror's truth.
Hence home-felt pleasure prompts the Patriot's sigh;

This makes him wish to live, and dare to die.
For this young FOSCAKI, whose hapless fate
Venice should blush to hear the Muse relate,
When exile wore his blooming years away,
To sorrow's long soliloquies a prey,
When reason, justice, vainly urg'd his cause,
For this he rous'd her sanguinary laws;
Glad to return, tho' Hope could grant no more,
And chains and torture hail'd him to the shore.
And hence the charm historic scenes impart:
Hence Tiber awes, and Avon melts the heart.
Aerial forms, in Tempe's classic vale,
Glance thro' the gloom, and whisper in the gale;
In wild Vaucluse with love and LAURA dwell,
And watch and weep in ELOISA'S cell.'
'Twas ever thus. As now at VIRGIL'S tomb,
We bless the shade, and bid the verdure bloom:
So TULLY paus'd, amid the wrecks of Time,
On the rude stone to trace the truth sublime;
When at his feet, in honour'd dust disclos'd,
The immortal Sage of Syracuse repos'd.
And as his youth in sweet delusion hung,
Where once a PLATO taught, a PINDAR sung;
Who now but meets him musing, when he roves
His ruin'd Tusculan's romantic groves?
In Rome's great forum, who but hears him roll
His moral thunders o'er the subject soul?
And hence that calm delight the portrait gives:
We gaze on every feature till it lives!
Still the fond lover views the absent maid;
And the lost friend still lingers in his shade!
Say why the pensive widow loves to weep,
When on her knee she rocks her babe to sleep:
Tremblingly still, she lifts his veil to trace
The father's features in his infant face.
The hoary grandsire smiles the hour away,
Won by the charm of Innocence at play;
He bends to meet each artless burst of joy,
Forgets his age, and acts again the boy.
What tho' the iron school of War erase
Each milder virtue, and each softer grace;
What tho' the fiend's torpedo-touch arrest
Each gentler, finer impulse of the breast;
Still shall this active principle preside,
And wake the tear to Pity's self denied.
The intrepid Swiss, that guards a foreign shore,
Condemn'd to climb his mountain-cliffs no more,
If chance he hears the song so sweetly wild
Which on those cliffs his infant hours beguil'd,
Melts at the long-lost scenes that round him rise,
And sinks a martyr to repentant sighs.

Ask not if courts or camps dissolve the charm:
Say why VESPASIAN lov'd his Sabine farm;
Why great NAVARRE, when France and freedom bled,
Sought the lone limits of a forest-shed.
When DIOCLETIAN'S self-corrected mind
The imperial fasces of a world resign'd,
Say why we trace the labours of his spade,
In calm Salona's philosophic shade.
Say, when contentious CHARLES renounc'd a throne,
To muse with monks unletter'd and unknown,
What from his soul the parting tribute drew?
What claim'd the sorrows of a last adieu?
The still retreats that sooth'd his tranquil breast,
Ere grandeur dazzled, and its cares oppress'd.
Undamp'd by time, the generous Instinct glows
Far as Angola's sands, as Zembla's snows;
Glows in the tiger's den, the serpent's nest,
On every form of varied life imprest.
The social tribes its choicest influence hail:
And, when the drum beats briskly in the gale,
The war-worn courser charges at the sound,
And with young vigour wheels the pasture round.
Oft has the aged tenant of the vale
Lean'd on his staff to lengthen out the tale;
Oft have his lips the grateful tribute breath'd,
From sire to son with pious zeal bequeath'd.
When o'er the blasted heath the day declin'd,
And on the scath'd oak warr'd the winter-wind;
When not a distant taper's twinkling ray
Gleam'd o'er the furze to light him on his way;
When not a sheep-bell sooth'd his listening ear,
And the big rain-drops told the tempest near;
Then did his horse the homeward track descry,
The track that shunn'd his sad, inquiring eye;
And win each wavering purpose to relent,
With warmth so mild, so gently violent,
That his charm'd hand the careless rein resign'd,
And doubts and terrors vanish'd from his mind.
Recall the traveller, whose alter'd form
Has borne the buffet of the mountain-storm;
And who will first his fond impatience meet?
His faithful dog's already at his feet!
Yes, tho' the porter spurn him from the door,
Tho' all, that knew him, know his face no more,
His faithful dog shall tell his joy to each,
With that mute eloquence which passes speech.
And see, the master but returns to die!
Yet who shall bid the watchful servant fly?
The blasts of heav'n, the drenching dews of earth,
The wanton insults of unfeeling mirth,
These, when to guard Misfortune's sacred grave,

Will firm Fidelity exult to brave.
Led by what chart, transports the timid dove
The wreaths of conquest, or the vows of love?
Say, thro' the clouds what compass points her flight?
Monarchs have gaz'd, and nations bless'd the sight.
Pile rocks on rocks, bid woods and mountains rise,
Eclipse her native shades, her native skies;
'Tis vain! thro' Ether's pathless wilds she goes,
And lights at last where all her cares repose.
Sweet bird! thy truth shall Harlem's walls attest,
And unborn ages consecrate thy nest.
When, with the silent energy of grief,
With looks that ask'd, yet dar'd not hope relief,
Want, with her babes, round generous Valour clung,
To wring the slow surrender from his tongue,
'Twas thine to animate her closing eye;
Alas! 'twas thine perchance the first to die,
Crush'd by her meagre hand, when welcom'd from the sky.
Hark! the bee winds her small but mellow horn,
Blithe to salute the sunny smile of morn.
O'er thymy downs she bends her busy course,
And many a stream allures her to its source.
'Tis noon, 'tis night. That eye so finely wrought,
Beyond the search of sense, the soar of thought.
Now vainly asks the scenes she left behind;
Its orb so full, its vision so confin'd!
Who guides the patient pilgrim to her cell?
Who bids her soul with conscious triumph swell?
With conscious truth retrace the mazy clue
Of varied scents, that charm'd her as she flew?
Hail, MEMORY, hail! thy universal reign
Guards the least link of Being's glorious chain.


THE PLEASURES OF MEMORY

PART II

Delle cose custode, e dispensiera.
*TASSO*

ANALYSIS OF THE SECOND PART

The Memory has hitherto acted only in subservience to the senses, and so far man is not eminently distinguished from other animals: but, with respect to man, she has a higher province; and is often busily employed, when excited by no external cause whatever. She preserves, for his use, the treasures of art and science, history and philosophy. She colours all the prospects of life: for 'we can only anticipate the future, by concluding what is possible from what is past.' On her agency depends every effusion of the Fancy, whose boldest effort can only compound or transpose, augment or diminish the materials which she has collected and retained.

When the first emotions of despair have subsided, and sorrow has softened into melancholy, she amuses with a retrospect of innocent pleasures, and inspires that noble confidence which results from the consciousness of having acted well. When sleep has suspended the organs of sense from their office, she not only supplies the mind with images, but assists in their combination. And even in madness itself, when the soul is resigned over to the tyranny of a distempered imagination, she revives past perceptions, and awakens the train of thought which was formerly most familiar.

Nor are we pleased only with a review of the brighter passages of life. Events, the most distressing in their immediate consequences, are often cherished in remembrance with a degree of enthusiasm.

But the world and its occupations give a mechanical impulse to the passions, which is not very favourable to the indulgence of this feeling. It is in a calm and well-regulated mind that the Memory is most perfect; and solitude is her best sphere of action. With this sentiment is introduced a Tale, illustrative of her influence in solitude, sickness, and, sorrow. And the subject having now been considered, so far as it relates to man and the animal world, the Poem concludes with a conjecture, that superior beings are blest with a nobler exercise of this faculty.


Sweet MEMORY, wafted by thy gentle gale,
Oft up the stream of Time I turn my sail,
To view the fairy-haunts of long-lost hours,
Blest with far greener shades, far fresher flowers.
Ages and climes remote to Thee impart
What charms in Genius, and refines in Art;
Thee, in whose hand the keys of Science dwell,
The pensive portress of her holy cell;
Whose constant vigils chase the chilling damp
Oblivion steals upon her vestal-lamp.
The friends of Reason, and the guides of Youth,
Whose language breath'd the eloquence of Truth;
Whose life, beyond preceptive wisdom, taught
The great in conduct, and the pure in thought;
These still exist, by Thee to Fame consign'd,
Still speak and act, the models of mankind.
From Thee sweet Hope her airy colouring draws;
And Fancy's flights are subject to thy laws.
From Thee that bosom-spring of rapture flows,
Which only Virtue, tranquil Virtue, knows.
When Joy's bright sun has shed his evening ray,
And Hope's delusive meteors cease to play;
When clouds on clouds the smiling prospect close,
Still thro' the gloom thy star serenely glows;
Like yon fair orb, she gilds the brow of night
With the mild magic of reflected light.
The beauteous maid, that bids the world adieu,
Oft of that world will snatch a fond review;
Oft at the shrine neglect her beads,
to trace Some social scene, some dear, familiar face,
Forgot, when first a father's stern controul
Chas'd the gay visions of her opening soul:

And ere, with iron tongue, the vesper-bell
Bursts thro' the cypress-walk, the convent-cell,
Oft will her warm and wayward heart revive,
To love and joy still tremblingly alive;
The whisper'd vow, the chaste caress prolong,
Weave the light dance and swell the choral song;
With rapt ear drink the enchanting serenade,
And, as it melts along the moonlight-glade,
To each soft note return as soft a sigh,
And bless the youth that bids her slumbers fly.
But not till Time has calm'd the ruffled breast,
Are these fond dreams of happiness confest.
Not till the rushing winds forget to rave,
Is Heav'n's sweet smile reflected on the wave.
From Guinea's coast pursue the lessening sail,
And catch the sounds that sadden every gale.
Tell, if thou canst, the sum of sorrows there;
Mark the fixt gaze, the wild and frenzied glare,
The racks of thought, and freezings of despair!
But pause not then beyond the western wave,
Go, view the captive barter'd as a slave!
Crush'd till his high, heroic spirit bleeds,
And from his nerveless frame indignantly recedes.
Yet here, ev'n here, with pleasures long resign'd,
Lo! MEMORY bursts the twilight of the mind:
Her dear delusions sooth his sinking soul,
When the rude scourge presumes its base controul;
And o'er Futurity's blank page diffuse
The full reflection of her vivid hues.
'Tis but to die, and then, to weep no more,
Then will he wake on Congo's distant shore;
Beneath his plantain's antient shade, renew
The simple transports that with freedom flew;
Catch the cool breeze that musky Evening blows,
And quaff the palm's rich nectar as it glows;
The oral tale of elder time rehearse,
And chant the rude, traditionary verse;
With those, the lov'd companions of his youth,
When life was luxury, and friendship truth.
Ah! why should Virtue fear the frowns of Fate?
Hers what no wealth can win, no power create!
A little world of clear and cloudless day,
Nor wreck'd by storms, nor moulder'd by decay;
A world, with MEMORY'S ceaseless sun-shine blest,
The home of Happiness, an honest breast.
But most we mark the wonders of her reign,
When Sleep has lock'd the senses in her chain.
When sober Judgment has his throne resign'd,
She smiles away the chaos of the mind;
And, as warm Fancy's bright Elysium glows,
From Her each image springs, each colour flows.

She is the sacred guest! the immortal friend!
Oft seen o'er sleeping Innocence to bend,
In that dead hour of night to Silence giv'n,
Whispering seraphic visions of her heav'n.
When the blithe son of Savoy, journeying round
With humble wares and pipe of merry sound,
From his green vale and shelter'd cabin hies,
And scales the Alps to visit foreign skies;
Tho' far below the forked lightnings play,
And at his feet the thunder dies away,
Oft, in the saddle rudely rock'd to sleep,
While his mule browses on the dizzy steep,
With MEMORY'S aid, he sits at home, and sees
His children sport beneath their native, trees,
And bends, to hear their cherub-voices call,
O'er the loud fury of the torrent's fall.
But can her smile with gloomy Madness dwell?
Say, can she chase the horrors of his cell?
Each fiery flight on Frenzy's wing restrain,
And mould the coinage of the fever'd brain?
Pass but that grate, which scarce a gleam supplies,
There in the dust the wreck of Genius lies!
He, whose arresting hand sublimely wrought
Each bold conception in the sphere of thought;
And round, in colours of the rainbow, threw
Forms ever fair, creations ever new!
But, as he fondly snatch'd the wreath of Fame,
The spectre Poverty unnerv'd his frame.
Cold was her grasp, a withering scowl she wore;
And Hope's soft energies were felt no more.
Yet still how sweet the soothings of his art!
From the rude wall what bright ideas start!
Ev'n now he claims the amaranthine wreath,
With scenes that glow, with images that breathe!
And whence these scenes, these images, declare.
Whence but from Her who triumphs o'er despair?
Awake, arise! with grateful fervor fraught,
Go, spring the mine of elevating thought.
He, who, thro' Nature's various walk, surveys
The good and fair her faultless line pourtrays;
Whose mind, prophan'd by no unhallow'd guest,
Culls from the crowd the purest and the best;
May range, at will, bright Fancy's golden clime,
Or, musing, mount where Science sits sublime,
Or wake the spirit of departed Time.
Who acts thus wisely, mark the moral muse,
A blooming Eden in his life reviews!
So rich the culture, tho' so small the space,
Its scanty limits he forgets to trace.
But the fond fool, when evening shades the sky,
Turns but to start, and gazes but to sigh!

The weary waste, that lengthen'd as he ran,
Fades to a blank, and dwindles to a span!
Ah! who can tell the triumphs of the mind,
By truth illumin'd, and by taste refin'd?
When Age has quench'd the eye and clos'd the ear,
Still nerv'd for action in her native sphere,
Oft will she rise with searching glance pursue
Some long-lov'd image vanish'd from her view;
Dart thro' the deep recesses of the past,
O'er dusky forms in chains of slumber cast;
With giant-grasp fling back the folds of night,
And snatch the faithless fugitive to light.
So thro' the grove the impatient mother flies.
Each sunless glade, each secret pathway tries;
Till the light leaves the truant boy disclose,
Long on the wood-moss stretch'd in sweet repose.
Nor yet to pleasing objects are confin'd
The silent feasts of the reflecting mind.
Danger and death a dread delight inspire;
And the bald veteran glows with wonted fire,
When, richly bronz'd by many a summer-sun,
He counts his scars, and tells what deeds were done.
Go, with old Thames, view Chelsea's glorious pile;
And ask the shatter'd hero, whence his smile?
Go, view the splendid domes of Greenwich - Go,
And own what raptures from Reflection flow.
Hail, noblest structures imag'd in the wave!
A nation's grateful tribute to the brave.
Hail, blest retreats from war and shipwreck, hail!
That oft arrest the wondering stranger's sail.
Long have ye heard the narratives of age,
The battle's havoc, and the tempest's rage;
Long have ye known Reflection's genial ray
Gild the calm close of Valour's various day.
Time's sombrous touches soon correct the piece,
Mellow each tint, and bid each discord cease:
A softer tone of light pervades the whole,
And steals a pensive languor o'er the soul.
Hast thou thro' Eden's wild-wood vales pursued
Each mountain-scene, majestically rude;
To note the sweet simplicity of life,
Far from the din of Folly's idle strife:
Nor there awhile, with lifted eye, rever'd
That modest stone which pious PEMBROKE rear'd;
Which still records, beyond the pencil's power,
The silent sorrows of a parting hour;
Still to the musing pilgrim points the place,
Her sainted spirit most delights to trace?
Thus, with the manly glow of honest pride,
O'er his dead son the gallant ORMOND sigh'd.
Thus, thro' the gloom of SHENSTONE'S fairy grove,

MARIA'S urn still breathes the voice of love.
As the stern grandeur of a Gothic tower
Awes us less deeply in its morning hour,
Than when the shades of Time serenely fall
On every broken arch and ivy'd wall;
The tender images we love to trace,
Steal from each year a melancholy grace!
And as the sparks of social love expand,
As the heart opens in a foreign land;
And, with a brother's warmth, a brother's smile,
The stranger greets each native of his isle;
So scenes of life, when present and confest,
Stamp but their bolder features on the breast;
Yet not an image, when remotely view'd,
However trivial, and however rude,
But wins the heart, and wakes the social sigh,
With every claim of close affinity!
But these pure joys the world can never know;
In gentler climes their silver currents flow.
Oft at the silent, shadowy close of day,
When the hush'd grove has sung its parting lay;
When pensive Twilight, in her dusky car,
Comes slowly on to meet the evening-star;
Above, below, aerial murmurs swell,
From hanging wood, brown heath, and bushy dell!
A thousand nameless rills, that shun the light,
Stealing soft music on the ear of night.
So oft the finer movements of the soul,
That shun the sphere of Pleasure's gay controul,
In the still shades of calm Seclusion rise,
And breathe their sweet, seraphic harmonies!
Once, and domestic annals tell the time,
(Preserv'd in Cumbria's rude, romantic clime)
When nature smil'd, and o'er the landscape threw
Her richest fragrance, and her brightest hue,
A blithe and blooming Forester explor'd
Those loftier scenes SALVATOR'S soul ador'd;
The rocky pass half hung with shaggy wood,
And the cleft oak flung boldly o'er the flood;
Nor shunn'd the path, unknown to human tread,
That downward to the night of caverns led;
Some antient cataract's deserted bed.
High on exulting wing the heath-cock rose,
And blew his shrill blast o'er perennial snows
Ere the rapt youth, recoiling from the roar,
Gaz'd on the tumbling tide of dread Lodoar;
And thro' the rifted cliffs, that scal'd the sky,
Derwent's clear mirror charm'd his dazzled eye.
Each osier isle, inverted on the wave,
Thro' morn's gray mist its melting colours gave;
And, o'er the cygnet's haunt, the mantling grove

Its emerald arch with wild luxuriance wove.
Light as the breeze that brush'd the orient dew:
From rock to rock the young adventurer flew;
And day's last sunshine slept along the shore,
When lo, a path the smile of welcome wore.
Imbowering shrubs with verdure veil'd the sky,
And on the musk-rose shed a deeper dye;
Save when a bright and momentary gleam
Glanc'd from the white foam of some shelter'd stream.
O'er the still lake the bell of evening toll'd,
And on the moor the shepherd penn'd his fold;
And on the green hill's side the meteor play'd;
When, hark! a voice sung sweetly thro' the shade.
It ceas'd yet still in FLORIO'S fancy sung,
Still on each note his captive spirit hung;
Till o'er the mead a cool, sequester'd grot
From its rich roof a sparry lustre shot.
A crystal water cross'd the pebbled floor,
And on the front these simple lines it bore:
Hence away, nor dare intrude!
In this secret, shadowy cell
Musing MEMORY loves to dwell,
With her sister Solitude.
Far from the busy world she flies,
To taste that peace the world denies.
Entranc'd she sits; from youth to age,
Reviewing Life's eventful page;
And noting, ere they fade away,
The little lines of yesterday.
FLORIO had gain'd a rude and rocky seat,
When lo, the Genius of this still retreat!
Fair was her form but who can hope to trace
The pensive softness of her angel-face?
Can VIRGIL'S verse, can RAPHAEL'S touch impart
Those finer features of the feeling heart,
Those tend'rer tints that shun the careless eye,
And in the world's contagious climate die?
She left the cave, nor mark'd the stranger there;
Her pastoral beauty, and her artless air
Had breath'd a soft enchantment o'er his soul!
In every nerve he felt her blest controul!
What pure and white-wing'd agents of the sky,
Who rule the springs of sacred sympathy,
Inform congenial spirits when they meet?
Sweet is their office, as their natures sweet!
FLORIO, with fearful joy, pursued the maid,
Till thro' a vista's moonlight-checquer'd shade,
Where the bat circled, and the rooks repos'd,
(Their wars suspended, and their councils clos'd)
An antique mansion burst in awful state,
A rich vine clustering round the Gothic gate.

Nor paus'd he there. The master of the scene
Saw his light step imprint the dewy green;
And, slow-advancing, hail'd him as his guest,
Won by the honest warmth his looks express'd,
He wore the rustic manners of a 'Squire;
Age had not quench'd one spark of manly fire;
But giant Gout had bound him in her chain,
And his heart panted for the chase in vain.
Yet here Remembrance, sweetly-soothing power!
Wing'd with delight Confinement's lingering hour.
The fox's brush still emulous to wear,
He scour'd the county in his elbow-chair;
And, with view-halloo, rous'd the dreaming hound,
That rung, by starts, his deep-ton'd music round.
Long by the paddock's humble pale confin'd,
His aged hunters cours'd the viewless wind:
And each, with glowing energy pourtray'd,
The far-fam'd triumphs of the field display'd:
Usurp'd the canvas of the crowded hall,
And chas'd a line of heroes from the wall.
There slept the horn each jocund echo knew.
And many a smile and many a story drew!
High o'er the hearth his forest-trophies hung,
And their fantastic branches wildly flung.
How would he dwell on the vast antlers there!
These dash'd the wave, those fann'd the mountain-air.
All, as they frown'd, unwritten records bore,
Of gallant feats and festivals of yore.
But why the tale prolong? His only child,
His darling JULIA on the stranger smil'd.
Her little arts a fretful sire to please,
Her gentle gaiety, and native ease
Had won his soul; and rapturous Fancy shed
Her golden lights, and tints of rosy red.
But ah! few days had pass'd, ere the bright vision fled!
When evening ting'd the lake's ethereal blue,
And her deep shades irregularly threw;
Their shifting sail dropt gently from the cove,
Down by St. Herbert's consecrated grove;
Whence erst the chanted hymn, the taper'd rite
Amus'd the fisher's solitary night:
And still the mitred window, richly wreath'd,
A sacred calm thro' the brown foliage breath'd.
The wild deer, starting thro' the silent glade,
With fearful gaze their various course survey'd.
High hung in air the hoary goat reclin'd,
His streaming beard the sport of every wind;
And, while the coot her jet-wing lov'd to lave,
Rock'd on the bosom of the sleepless wave;
The eagle rush'd from Skiddaw's purple crest,
A cloud still brooding o'er her giant-nest.

And now the moon had dimm'd, with dewy ray.
The few fine flushes of departing day;
O'er the wide water's deep serene she hung,
And her broad lights on every mountain flung;
When lo! a sudden blast the vessel blew,
And to the surge consign'd the little crew.
All, all escap'd but ere the lover bore
His faint and faded JULIA, to the shore,
Her sense had fled! Exhausted by the storm,
A fatal trance hang o'er her pallid form;
Her closing eye a trembling lustre fir'd;
'Twas life's last spark, it flutter'd and expir'd!
The father strew'd his white hairs in the wind,
Call'd on his child, nor linger'd long behind:
And FLORIO liv'd to see the willow wave,
With many an evening-whisper, o'er their grave.
Yes, FLORIO liv'd and, still of each possest,
The father cherish'd, and the maid caress'd!
For ever would the fond enthusiast rove,
With JULIA'S spirit, thro' the shadowy grove;
Gaze with delight on every scene she plann'd,
Kiss every flowret planted by her hand.
Ah! still he trac'd her steps along the glade,
When hazy hues and glimmering lights betray'd
Half-viewless forms; still listen'd as the breeze
Heav'd its deep sobs among the aged trees;
And at each pause her melting accents caught,
In sweet delirium of romantic thought!
Dear was the grot that shunn'd the blaze of day;
She gave its spars to shoot a trembling ray.
The spring, that bubbled from its inmost cell,
Murmur'd of JULIA'S virtues as it fell;
And o'er the dripping moss, the fretted stone,
In FLORIO'S ear breath'd language not its own.
Her charm around the enchantress MEMORY threw,
A charm that sooths the mind, and sweetens too!
But is Her magic only felt below?
Say, thro' what brighter realms she bids it flow;
To what pure beings, in a nobler sphere,
She yields delight but faintly imag'd here:
All that till now their rapt researches knew,
Not call'd in slow succession to review;
But, as a landscape meets the eye of day,
At once presented to their glad survey!
Each scene of bliss reveal'd, since chaos fled,
And dawning light its dazzling glories spread;
Each chain of wonders that sublimely glow'd,
Since first Creation's choral anthem flow'd;
Each ready flight, at Mercy's smile divine,
To distant worlds that undiscover'd shine;
Full on her tablet flings its living rays,

And all, combin'd, with blest effulgence blaze.
There thy bright train, immortal Friendship, soar;
No more to part, to mingle tears no more!
And, as the softening hand of Time endears
The joys and sorrows of our infant-years,
So there the soul, releas'd from human strife,
Smiles at the little cares and ills of life;
Its lights and shades, its sunshine and its showers;
As at a dream that charm'd her vacant hours!
Oft may the spirits of the dead descend
To watch the silent slumbers of a friend;
To hover round his evening-walk unseen,
And hold sweet converse on the dusky green;
To hail the spot where first their friendship grew,
And heav'n and nature open'd to their view!
Oft, when he trims his cheerful hearth, and sees
A smiling circle emulous to please;
There may these gentle guests delight to dwell,
And bless the scene they lov'd in life so well!
Oh thou! with whom my heart was wont to share
From Reason's dawn each pleasure and each care;
With whom, alas! I fondly hop'd to know
The humble walks of happiness below;
If thy blest nature now unites above
An angel's pity with a brother's love,
Still o'er my life preserve thy mild controul,
Correct my views, and elevate my soul;
Grant me thy peace and purity of mind,
Devout yet cheerful, active yet resign'd;
Grant me, like thee, whose heart knew no disguise,
Whose blameless wishes never aim'd to rise,
To meet the changes Time and Chance present,
With modest dignity and calm content.
When thy last breath, ere Nature sunk to rest,
Thy meek submission to thy God express'd;
When thy last look, ere thought and feeling fled,
A mingled gleam of hope and triumph shed;
What to thy soul its glad assurance gave,
Its hope in death, its triumph o'er the grave?
The sweet Remembrance of unblemish'd youth,
The still inspiring voice of Innocence and Truth!
Hail, MEMORY, hail! in thy exhaustless mine
From age to age unnumber'd treasures shine!
Thought and her shadowy brood thy call obey,
And Place and Time are subject to thy sway!
Thy pleasures most we feel, when most alone;
The only pleasures we can call our own.
Lighter than air, Hope's summer-visions die,
If but a fleeting cloud obscure the sky;
If but a beam of sober Reason play,
Lo, Fancy's fairy frost-work melts away!

But can the wiles of Art, the grasp of Power,
Snatch the rich relics of a well-spent hour?
These, when the trembling spirit wings her flight,
Pour round her path a stream of living light;
And gild those pure and perfect realms of rest,
Where Virtue triumphs, and her sons are blest!


## AN EPISTLE TO A FRIEND

*Villula,..........et pauper agelle,*
*Me tibi, et hos unâ mecum, et quos semper amavi,*
*Commendo.*


## PREFACE

Every reader turns with pleasure to those passages of Horace, and Pope, and Boileau, which describe how they lived and where they dwelt; and which, being interspersed among their satirical writings, derive a secret and irresistible grace from the contrast, and are admirable examples of what in Painting is termed repose.

We have admittance to Horace at all hours. We enjoy the company and conversation at his table; and his suppers, like Plato's, 'non solum in præsentia, sed etiam postero die jucundæ sunt.' But when we look round as we sit there, we find ourselves in a Sabine farm, and not in a Roman villa. His windows have every charm of prospect; but his furniture might have descended from Cincin-natus; and gems, and pictures, and old marbles, are mentioned by him more than once with a seeming indifference.

His English Imitator thought and felt, perhaps, more correctly on the subject; and embellished his garden and grotto with great industry and success. But to these alone he solicits our notice. On the ornaments of his house he is silent; and he appears to have reserved all the minuter touches of his pencil for the library, the chapel, and the banquetting-room of Timon. 'Le savoir de notre siècle,' says Rousseau, 'tend beaucoup plus à détruire qu'à edifier. On censure d'un ton de maitre; pour proposer, il en faut prendre un autre.'

It is the design of this Epistle to illustrate the virtue of True Taste; and to shew how little she requires to secure, not only the comforts, but even the elegancies of life. True Taste is an excellent Economist. She confines her choice to few objects, and delights in producing great effects by small means: while False Taste is for ever sighing after the new and the rare; and reminds us, in her works, of the Scholar of Apelles, who, not being able to paint his Helen beautiful, determined to make her fine.


## ARGUMENT

*An Invitation, v. 1. The approach to a Villa described, v. 5. Its situation, v. 17. Its few apartments, v. 57. Furnished with casts from the Antique, &c. v. 63. The dining-room, v. 83. The library, v. 89. A cold-*

When, with a REAUMUR'S skill, thy curious mind
Has class'd the insect-tribes of human-kind,
Each with its busy hum, or gilded wing,
Its subtle, web-work, or its venom'd sting;
Let me, to claim a few unvalued hours,
Point the green lane that leads thro' fern and flowers;
The shelter'd gate that opens to my field,
And the white front thro' mingling elms reveal'd.
In vain, alas, a village-friend invites
To simple comforts, and domestic rites,
When the gay months of Carnival resume
Their annual round of glitter and perfume;
When London hails thee to its splendid mart,
Its hives of sweets, and cabinets of art;
And, lo, majestic as thy manly song,
Flows the full tide of human life along.
Still must my partial pencil love to dwell
On the home-prospects of my hermit cell;
The mossy pales that skirt the orchard-green,
Here hid by shrub-wood, there by glimpses seen;
And the brown pathway, that, with careless flow,
Sinks, and is lost among the trees below.
Still must it trace (the flattering tints forgive)
Each fleeting charm that bids the landscape live.
Oft o'er the mead, at pleasing distance, pass
Browsing the hedge by fits the pannier'd ass;
The idling shepherd-boy, with rude delight,
Whistling his dog to mark the pebble's flight;
And in her kerchief blue the cottage-maid,
With brimming pitcher from the shadowy glade.
Far to the south a mountain-vale retires,
Rich in its groves, and glens, and village-spires;
Its upland lawns, and cliffs with foliage hung,
Its wizard-stream, nor nameless nor unsung:
And thro' the various year, the various day,
What scenes of glory burst, and melt away!
When April-verdure springs in Grosvenor-square,
And the furr'd Beauty comes to winter there,
She bids old Nature mar the plan no more;
Yet still the seasons circle as before.
Ah, still as soon the young Aurora plays,
Tho' moons and flambeaux trail their broadest blaze;
As soon the sky-lark pours his matin song,
Tho' Evening lingers at the mask so long.
There let her strike with momentary ray,
As tapers shine their little lives away;
There let her practise from herself to steal,
And look the happiness she does not feel;

The ready smile and bidden blush employ
At Faro-routs that dazzle to destroy;
Fan with affected ease the essenc'd air,
And lisp of fashions with unmeaning stare.
Be thine to meditate an humbler flight,
When morning fills the fields with rosy light;
Be thine to blend, nor thine a vulgar aim,
Repose with dignity, with Quiet fame.
Here no state-chambers in long line unfold,
Bright with broad mirrors, rough with fretted gold;
Yet modest ornament, with use combin'd,
Attracts the eye to exercise the mind.
Small change of scene, small space his home requires,
Who leads a life of satisfied desires.
What tho' no marble breathes, no canvass glows,
From every point a ray of genius flows!
Be mine to bless the more mechanic skill,
That stamps, renews, and multiplies at will;
And cheaply circulates, thro' distant climes,
The fairest relics of the purest times.
Here from the mould to conscious being start
Those finer forms, the miracles of art;
Here chosen gems, imprest on sulphur, shine,
That slept for ages in a second mine;
And here the faithful graver dares to trace
A MICHAEL'S grandeur, and a RAPHAEL'S grace!
Thy gallery, Florence, gilds my humble walls,
And my low roof the Vatican recalls!
Soon as the morning-dream my pillow flies,
To waking sense what brighter visions rise!
O mark! again the coursers of the Sun,
At GUIDO'S call, their round of glory run!
Again the rosy Hours resume their flight,
Obscur'd and lost in floods of golden light!
But could thine erring friend so long forget
(Sweet source of pensive joy and fond regret)
That here its warmest hues the pencil flings,
Lo! here the lost restores, the absent brings;
And still the Few best lov'd and most rever'd
Rise round the board their social smile endear'd?
Selected shelves shall claim thy studious hours;
There shall thy ranging mind be fed on flowers!
There, while the shaded lamp's mild lustre streams,
Read antient books, or woo inspiring dreams;
And, when a sage's bust arrests thee there,
Pause, and his features with his thoughts compare.
Ah, most that Art my grateful rapture calls,
Which breathes a soul into the silent walls;
Which gathers round the Wise of every Tongue,
All on whose words departed nations hung;
Still prompt to charm with many a converse sweet;

Guides in the world, companions in retreat!
Tho' my thatch'd bath no rich Mosaic knows,
A limpid spring with unfelt current flows.
Emblem of Life! which, still as we survey,
Seems motionless, yet ever glides away!
The shadowy walls record, with Attic art,
The strength and beauty that its waves impart.
Here THETIS, bending, with a mother's fears
Dips her dear boy, whose pride restrains his tears.
There, VENUS, rising, shrinks with sweet surprize,
As her fair self reflected seems to rise!
Far from the joyless glare, the maddening strife,
And all 'the dull impertinence of life,'
These eyelids open to the rising ray,
And close, when Nature bids, at close of day.
Here, at the dawn, the kindling landscape glows;
There noon-day levees call from faint repose.
Here the flush'd wave flings back the parting light;
There glimmering lamps anticipate the night.
When from his classic dreams the student steals,
Amid the buzz of crowds, the whirl of wheels,
To muse unnotic'd while around him press
The meteor-forms of equipage and dress;
Alone, in wonder lost, he seems to stand
A very stranger in his native land!
And (tho' perchance of current coin possest,
And modern phrase by living lips exprest)
Like those blest Youths, forgive the fabling page,
Whose blameless lives deceiv'd a twilight age,
Spent in sweet slumbers; till the miner's spade
Unclos'd the cavern, and the morning play'd.
Ah, what their strange surprize, their wild delight!
New arts of life, new manners meet their sight!
In a new world they wake, as from the dead;
Yet doubt the trance dissolv'd, the vision fled!
O come, and, rich in intellectual wealth,
Blend thought with exercise, with knowledge health!
Long, in this shelter'd scene of letter'd talk,
With sober step repeat the pensive walk;
Nor scorn, when graver triflings fail to please,
The cheap amusements of a mind at ease;
Here every care in sweet oblivion cast,
And many an idle hour not idly pass'd.
No tuneful echoes, ambush'd at my gate,
Catch the blest accents of the wise and great.
Vain of its various page, no Album breathes
The sigh that Friendship or the Muse bequeaths.
Yet some good Genii o'er my hearth preside,
Oft the far friend, with secret spell, to guide;
And there I trace, when the grey evening lours,
A silent chronicle of happier hours!

When Christmas revels in a world of snow,
And bids her berries blush, her carols flow;
His spangling shower when Frost the wizard flings;
Or, borne in ether blue, on viewless wings,
O'er the white pane his silvery foliage weaves,
And gems with icicles the sheltering eaves;
Thy muffled friend his nectarine-wall pursues,
What time the sun the yellow crocus wooes,
Screen'd from the arrowy North; and duly hies
To meet the morning-rumour as it flies;
To range the murmuring market-place, and view
The motley groups that faithful TENIERS drew.
When Spring bursts forth in blossoms thro' the vale,
And her wild music triumphs on the gale,
Oft with my book I muse from stile to stile;
Oft in my porch the listless noon beguile,
Framing loose numbers, till declining day
Thro' the green trellis shoots a crimson ray;
Till the West-wind leads on the twilight hours,
And shakes the fragrant bells of closing flowers.
Nor boast, O Choisy! seat of soft delight,
The secret charm of thy voluptuous night.
Vain is the blaze of wealth, the pomp of power!
Lo, here, attendant on the shadowy hour,
Thy closet-supper, serv'd by hands unseen,
Sheds, like an evening-star, its ray serene,
To hail our coming. Not a step prophane
Dares, with rude sound, the cheerful rite restrain;
And, while the frugal banquet glows reveal'd,
Pure and unbought, the natives of my field;
While blushing fruits thro' scatter'd leaves invite,
Still clad in bloom, and veil'd in azure light;
With wine, as rich in years as HORACE sings,
With water, clear as his own fountain flings,
The shifting side-board plays its humbler part,
Beyond the triumphs of a Loriot's art.
Thus, in this calm recess, so richly fraught
With mental light, and luxury of thought,
My life steals on; (O could it blend with thine!)
Careless my course, yet not without design.
So thro' the vales of Loire the bee-hives glide,
The light raft dropping with the silent tide;
So, till the laughing scenes are lost in night,
The busy people wing their various flight,
Culling unnumber'd sweets from nameless flowers,
That scent the vineyard in its purple hours.
Rise, ere the watch-relieving clarions play,
Caught thro' St. James's groves at blush of day;
Ere its full voice the choral anthem flings
Thro' trophied tombs of heroes and of kings.
Haste to the tranquil shade of learned ease,

Tho' skill'd alike to dazzle and to please;
Tho' each gay scene be search'd with anxious eye,
Nor thy shut door be pass'd without a sigh.
If, when this roof shall know thy friend no more,
Some, form'd like thee, should once, like thee, explore;
Invoke the lares of his lov'd retreat,
And his lone walks imprint with pilgrim-feet;
Then be it said, (as, vain of better days,
Some grey domestic prompts the partial praise)
"Unknown he liv'd, unenvied, not unblest;
Reason his guide, and Happiness his guest.
In the clear mirror of his moral page,
We trace the manners of a purer age.
His soul, with thirst of genuine glory fraught,
Scorn'd the false lustre of licentious thought.
One fair asylum from the world he knew,
One chosen seat, that charms with various view!
Who boasts of more (believe the serious strain)
Sighs for a home, and sighs, alas! in vain.
Thro' each he roves, the tenant of a day,
And, with the swallow, wings the year away!"


ODE TO SUPERSTITION. [*1]

I. 1.
Hence, to the realms of Night, dire Demon, hence!
Thy chain of adamant can bind
That little world, the human mind,
And sink its noblest powers to impotence.
Wake the lion's loudest roar,
Clot his shaggy mane with gore,
With flashing fury bid his eye-balls shine;
Meek is his savage, sullen soul, to thine!
Thy touch, thy deadening touch has steel'd the breast, [*2]
Whence, thro' her April-shower, soft Pity smil'd;
Has clos'd the heart each godlike virtue bless'd,
To all the silent pleadings of his child.
At thy command he plants the dagger deep,
At thy command exults, tho' Nature bids him weep!

I. 2.
When, with a frown that froze the peopled earth,
Thou dartedst thy huge head from high,
Night wav'd her banners o'er the sky,
And, brooding, gave her shapeless shadows birth.
Rocking on the billowy air,
Ha! what withering phantoms glare!
As blows the blast with many a sudden swell,
At each dead pause, what shrill-ton'd voices yell!

The sheeted spectre, rising from the tomb,
Points at the murderer's stab, and shudders by;
In every grove is felt a heavier gloom,
That veils its genius from the vulgar eye:
The spirit of the water rides the storm,
And, thro' the mist, reveals the terrors of his form.

I. 3.
O'er solid seas, where Winter reigns,
And holds each mountain-wave in chains,
The fur-clad savage, ere he guides his deer [*3]
By glistering star-light thro' the snow,
Breathes softly in her wondering ear
Each potent spell thou bad'st him know.
By thee inspir'd, on India's sands, [*4]
Full in the sun the Bramin stands;
And, while the panting tigress hies
To quench her fever in the stream,
His spirit laughs in agonies, [*5]
Smit by the scorchings of the noontide beam.
Mark who mounts the sacred pyre,
Blooming in her bridal vest:
She hurls the torch! she fans the fire!
To die is to be blest: [*6]
She clasps her lord to part no more,
And, sighing, sinks! but sinks to soar.
O'ershadowing Scotia's desert coast,
The Sisters sail in dusky state, [*7]
And, wrapt in clouds, in tempests tost,
Weave the airy web of fate;
While the lone shepherd, near the shipless main, [*8]
Sees o'er her hills advance the long-drawn funeral train,

II. 1.
Thou spak'st, and lo! a new creation glow'd.
Each unhewn mass of living stone
Was clad in horrors not its own,
And at its base the trembling nations bow'd.
Giant Error, darkly grand,
Grasp'd the globe with iron hand.
Circled with seats of bliss, the Lord of Light
Saw prostrate worlds adore his golden height.
The statue, waking with immortal powers, [*9]
Springs from its parent earth, and shakes the spheres;
The indignant pyramid sublimely towers,
And braves the efforts of a host of years.
Sweet Music breathes her soul into the wind;
And bright-ey'd Painting stamps the image of the mind.

II. 2.
Round their rude ark old Egypt's sorcerers rise!

A timbrell'd anthem swells the gale,
And bids the God of Thunders hail; [*10]
With lowings loud the captive God replies.
Clouds of incense woo thy smile,
Scaly monarch of the Nile! [*11]
But ah! what myriads claim the bended knee? [*12]
Go, count the busy drops that swell the sea.
Proud land! what eye can trace thy mystic lore,
Lock'd up in characters as dark as night? [*13]
What eye those long, long labyrinths dare explore, [*14]
To which the parted soul oft wings her flight;
Again to visit her cold cell of clay,
Charm'd with perennial sweets, and smiling at decay?

II. 3.
On yon hoar summit, mildly bright [*15]
With purple ether's liquid light,
High o'er the world, the white-rob'd Magi gaze
On dazzling bursts of heavenly fire;
Start at each blue, portentous blaze,
Each flame that flits with adverse spire.
But say, what sounds my ear invade
From Delphi's venerable shade?
The temple rocks, the laurel waves!
"The God! the God!" the Sybil cries.
Her figure swells! she foams, she raves!
Her figure swells to more than mortal size!
Streams of rapture roll along,
Silver notes ascend the skies:
Wake, Echo, wake and catch the song,
Oh catch it, ere it dies!
The Sybil speaks, the dream is o'er,
The holy harpings charm no more.
In vain she checks the God's controul;
His madding spirit fills her frame,
And moulds the features of her soul,
Breathing a prophetic flame.
The cavern frowns;  its hundred mouths unclose!
And, In the thunder's voice, the fate of empire flows.

III. 1.
Mona, thy Druid-rites awake the dead!
Rites thy brown oaks would never dare
Ev'n whisper to the idle air;
Rites that have chain'd old Ocean on his bed.
Shiver'd by thy piercing glance,
Pointless falls the hero's lance.
Thy magic bids the imperial eagle fly,
And blasts the laureate wreath of victory.
Hark, the bard's soul inspires the vocal string!
At every pause dread Silence hovers o'er:

While murky Night sails round on raven-wing,
Deepening the tempest's howl, the torrent's roar;
Chas'd by the morn from Snowdon's awful brow,
Where late she sate and scowl'd on the black wave below.

III. 2.
Lo, steel-clad War his gorgeous standard rears!
The red-cross squadrons madly rage, [*16]
And mow thro' infancy and age:
Then kiss the sacred dust and melt in tears.
Veiling from the eye of day,
Penance dreams her life away;
In cloister'd solitude she sits and sighs,
While from each shrine still, small responses rise.
Hear, with what heart-felt beat, the midnight bell
Swings its slow summons thro' the hollow pile!
The weak, wan votarist leaves her twilight cell,
To walk, with taper dim, the winding isle;
With choral chantings vainly to aspire,
Beyond this nether sphere, on Rapture's wing of fire.

III. 3.
Lord of each pang the nerves can feel,
Hence, with the rack and reeking wheel.
Faith lifts the soul above this little ball!
While gleams of glory open round,
And circling choirs of angels call,
Can'st thou, with all thy terrors crown'd,
Hope to obscure that latent spark,
Destin'd to shine when suns are dark?
Thy triumphs cease! thro' every land,
Hark! Truth proclaims, thy triumphs cease:
Her heavenly form, with glowing hand,
Benignly points to piety and peace.
Flush'd with youth her looks impart
Each fine feeling as it flows;
Her voice the echo of her heart,
Pure as the mountain-snows:
Celestial transports round her play,
And softly, sweetly die away.
She smiles! and where is now the cloud
That blacken'd o'er thy baleful reign?
Grim darkness furls his leaden shroud,
Shrinking from her glance in vain.
Her touch unlocks the day-spring from above,
And lo! it visits man with beams of light and love.

*1: Written in the year 1784.
*2: An allusion to the sacrifice of Iphigenia.
*3: When we were ready to set out, our host muttered some words in the ears of our cattle. See a
Voyage to the North of Europe in 1653.

*4: The Bramins expose their bodies to the intense heat of the sun.

*5: Ridens moriar. The conclusion of an old Runic ode.

*6: In the Bedas, or sacred writings of the Hindoos, it is written: "She, who dies with her husband, shall live for ever with him in heaven."

*7: The Fates of the Northern Mythology. See MALLET'S Antiquities.

*8: An allusion to the Second Sight.

*9: See that fine description of the sudden animation of the Palladium in the second book of the Æneid.

*10: The bull, Apis.

*11: The Crocodile.

*12: So numerous were the Deities of Egypt, that, according to an antient proverb, it was in that country less difficult to find a god than a man.

*13: The Hieroglyphics.

*14: The Catacombs, in which the bodies of the earliest generations yet remain without corruption, by virtue of the gums that embalmed them.

*15: "The Persians," says Herodotus, "reject the use of temples, altars, and statues. The tops of the highest mountains are the places chosen for sacrifices." I. 131. The elements, and more particularly Fire, were the objects of their religious reverence.

*16: This remarkable event happened at the siege and sack of Jerusalem, in the last year of the eleventh century. Hume, I.221.


VERSES WRITTEN TO BE SPOKEN BY MRS. SIDDONS *

Yes, 'tis the pulse of life! my fears were vain!
I wake, I breathe, and am myself again.
Still in this nether world; no seraph yet!
Nor walks my spirit, when the sun is set,
With troubled step to haunt the fatal board,
Where I died last by poison or the sword;
Blanching each honest cheek with deeds of night,
Done here so oft by dim and doubtful light.
To drop all metaphor, that little bell
Call'd back reality, and broke the spell.
No heroine claims your tears with tragic tone;
A very woman, scarce restrains her own!
Can she, with fiction, charm the cheated mind,
When to be grateful is the part assign'd?
Ah, No! she scorns the trappings of her Art;
No theme but truth, no prompter but the heart!
But, Ladies, say, must I alone unmask?
Is here no other actress? let me ask.
Believe me, those, who best the heart dissect,
Know every Woman studies stage-effect.
She moulds her manners to the part she, fills,
As Instinct teaches, or as Humour wills;
And, as the grave or gay her talent calls,
Acts in the drama, till the curtain falls.
First, how her little breast with triumph swells,
When the red coral rings its golden bells!

To play in pantomime is then the rage,
Along the carpet's many-colour'd stage;
Or lisp her merry thoughts with loud endeavour,
Now here, now there, in noise and mischief ever!
A school-girl next, she curls her hair in papers,
And mimics father's gout, and mother's vapours;
Discards her doll, bribes Betty for romances;
Playful at church, and serious when she dances;
Tramples alike on customs and on toes,
And whispers all she hears to all she knows;
Terror of caps, and wigs, and sober notions!
A romp! that longest of perpetual motions!
Till tam'd and tortur'd into foreign graces,
She sports her lovely face at public places;
And with blue, laughing eyes, behind her fan,
First acts her part with that great actor, MAN.
Too soon a flirt, approach her and she flies!
Frowns when pursued, and, when entreated, sighs!
Plays with unhappy men as cats with mice;
Till fading beauty hints the late advice.
Her prudence dictates what her pride disdain'd,
And now she sues to slaves herself had chain'd!
Then comes that good old character, a Wife,
With all the dear, distracting cares of life;
A thousand cards a day at doors to leave,
And, in return, a thousand cards receive;
Rouge high, play deep, to lead the ton aspire,
With nightly blaze set PORTLAND-PLACE on fire;
Snatch half a glimpse at Concert, Opera, Ball,
A Meteor, trac'd by none, tho' seen by all;
And, when her shatter'd nerves forbid to roam,
In very spleen rehearse the girls at home.
Last the grey Dowager, in antient flounces,
With snuff and spectacles the age denounces;
Boasts how the Sires of this degenerate Isle
Knelt for a look, and duell'd for a smile.
The scourge and ridicule of Goth and Vandal,
Her tea she sweetens, as she sips, with scandal;
With modern Belles eternal warfare wages,
Like her own birds that clamour from their cages;
And shuffles round to bear her tale to all,
Like some old Ruin, 'nodding to its fall!'
Thus WOMAN makes her entrance and her exit;
Not least an actress, when she least suspects it.
Yet Nature oft peeps out and mars the plot,
Each lesson lost, each poor pretence forgot;
Full oft, with energy that scorns controul,
At once lights up the features of the soul;
Unlocks each thought chain'd by coward Art,
And to full day the latent passions start!
And she, whose first, best wish is your applause,

Herself exemplifies the truth she draws.
Born on the stage thro' every shifting scene,
Obscure or bright, tempestuous or serene,
Still has your smile her trembling spirit fir'd!
And can she act, with thoughts like these inspir'd?
Thus from her mind all artifice she flings,
All skill, all practice, now unmeaning things!
To you, uncheck'd, each genuine feeling flows;
For all that life endears to you she owes.

*After a Tragedy, performed for her benefit, at the Theatre Royal in Drury-lane, April 27, 1795.

To —

Go, you may call it madness, folly;
You shall not chase my gloom away.
There's such a charm in melancholy,
I would not, if I could, be gay.

Oh, if you knew the pensive pleasure
That fills my bosom when I sigh,
You would not rob me of a treasure
Monarchs are too poor to buy.

THE SAILOR

The Sailor sighs as sinks his native shore,
As all its lessening turrets bluely fade;
He climbs the mast to feast his eye once more,
And busy Fancy fondly lends her aid.

Ah! now, each dear, domestic scene he knew,
Recall'd and cherish'd in a foreign clime,
Charms with the magic of a moonlight-view;
Its colours mellow'd, not impair'd, by time,

True as the needle, homeward points his heart,
Thro' all the horrors of the stormy main;
This, the last wish that would with life depart,
To meet the smile of her he loves again.

When Morn first faintly draws her silver line,
Or Eve's grey cloud descends to drink the wave;
When sea and sky in midnight darkness join,
Still, still he views the parting look she gave.

Her gentle spirit, lightly hovering o'er,

Attends his little bark from pole to pole;
And, when the beating billows round him roar,
Whispers sweet hope to sooth his troubled soul.

Carv'd is her name in many a spicy grove,
In many a plaintain-forest, waving wide;
Where dusky youths in painted plumage rove,
And giant palms o'er-arch the golden tide.

But lo, at last he comes with crowded sail!
Lo, o'er the cliff what eager figures bend!
And hark, what mingled murmurs swell the gale!
In each he hears the welcome of a friend.

'Tis she, 'tis she herself! she waves her hand!
Soon is the anchor cast, the canvass furl'd;
Soon thro' the whitening surge he springs to land,
And clasps the maid he singled from the world.


TO AN OLD OAK

*Immota manet; multosque nepotes,*
*Multa virûm volvens durando sæcula, vincit.*
*VIRGIL*


Round thee, alas, no shadows move!
From thee no sacred murmurs breathe!
Yet within thee, thyself a grove,
Once did the eagle scream above,
And the wolf howl beneath.

There once the steel-clad knight reclin'd,
His sable plumage tempest-toss'd;
And, as the death-bell smote the wind,
From towers long fled by human kind,
His brow the hero cross'd!

Then Culture came, and days serene,
And village-sports, and garlands gay.
Full many a pathway cross'd the green;
And maids and shepherd-youths were seen,
To celebrate the May.

Father of many a forest deep,
(Whence many a navy thunder-fraught)
Erst in their acorn-cells asleep,
Soon destin'd o'er the world to sweep,
Opening new spheres of thought!

Wont in the night of woods to dwell,
The holy druid saw thee rise;
And, planting there the guardian-spell,
Sung forth, the dreadful pomp to swell
Of human sacrifice!

Thy singed top and branches bare
Now straggle in the evening sky;
And the wan moon wheels round to glare
On the long corse that shivers there
Of him who came to die!


FRAGMENTS FROM EURIPIDES

Dear is that valley to the murmuring bees.
The small birds build there; and, at summer-noon,
Oft have I heard a child, gay among flowers,
As in the shining grass she sate conceal'd,
Sing to herself.

There is a streamlet issuing from a rock.
The village-girls, singing wild madrigals,
Dip their white vestments in its waters clear,
And hang them to the sun. There first I saw her.
Her dark and eloquent eyes, mild, full of fire,
'Twas heav'n to look upon; and her sweet voice,
As tuneable as harp of many strings,
At once spoke joy and sadness to my soul!


TWO SISTERS*

Well may you sit within, and, fond of grief,
Look in each other's face, and melt in tears.
Well may you shun all counsel, all relief.
Oh she was great in mind, tho' young in years!

Chang'd is that lovely countenance, which shed
Light when she spoke; and kindled sweet surprise,
As o'er her frame each warm emotion spread,
Play'd round her lips, and sparkled in her eyes.

Those lips so pure, that mov'd but to persuade,
Still to the last enliven'd and endear'd.
Those eyes at once her secret soul convey'd,
And ever beam'd delight when you appear'd.

Yet has she fled the life of bliss below,
That youthful Hope in bright perspective drew?
False were the tints! false as the feverish glow
That o'er her burning cheek Distemper threw!

And now in joy she dwells, in glory moves!
(Glory and joy reserv'd for you to share.)
Far, far more blest in blessing those she loves,
Than they, alas! unconscious of her care.

*On the death of a younger sister.


## WRITTEN AT MIDNIGHT

1786

While thro' the broken pane the tempest sighs,
And my step falters on the faithless floor,
Shades of departed joys around me rise,
With many a face that smiles on me no more;
With many a voice that thrills of transport gave,
Now silent as the grass that tufts their grave!


## ON A TEAR

Oh! that the Chemist's magic art
Could crystallize this sacred treasure!
Long should it glitter near my heart,
A secret source of pensive pleasure.

The little brilliant, ere it fell,
Its lustre caught from CHLOE'S eye;
Then, trembling, left its coral cell
The spring of Sensibility!

Sweet drop of pure and pearly light!
In thee the rays of Virtue shine;
More calmly clear, more mildly bright,
Than any gem that gilds the mine.

Benign restorer of the soul!
Who ever fly'st to bring relief,
When first we feel the rude controul
Of Love or Pity, Joy or Grief.

The sage's and the poet's theme,
In every clime, in every age;

Thou charm'st in Fancy's idle dream,
In Reason's philosophic page.

That very law* which moulds a tear,
And bids it trickle from its source,
That law preserves the earth a sphere,
And guides the planets in their course.

*The Law of Gravitation.


TO A VOICE THAT HAD BEEN LOST

*Vane, quid affectas faciem mihi ponere, pictor?*
*Aëris et lingua sum filia;*
*Et, si vis similem pingere, pinge sonum.*
*AUSONIUS.*


Once more, Enchantress of the soul,
Once more we hail thy soft controul.
Yet whither, whither did'st thou fly?
To what bright region of the sky?
Say, in what distant star to dwell?
(Of other worlds thou seemst to tell)
Or trembling, fluttering here below,
Resolv'd and unresolv'd to go,
In secret didst thou still impart
Thy raptures to the Pure in heart?
Perhaps to many a desert shore,
Thee, in his rage, the Tempest bore;
Thy broken murmurs swept along,
Mid Echoes yet untun'd by song;
Arrested in the realms of Frost,
Or in the wilds of Ether lost.
Far happier thou! 'twas thine to soar,
Careering on the winged wind.
Thy triumphs who shall dare explore?
Suns and their systems left behind.
No tract of space, no distant star,
No shock of elements at war,
Did thee detain. Thy wing of fire
Bore thee amidst the Cherub-choir;
And there awhile to thee 'twas giv'n
Once more that Voice belov'd to join,
Which taught thee first a flight divine,
And nurs'd thy infant years with many a strain from Heav'n!

## FROM A GREEK EPIGRAM

While on the cliff with calm delight she kneels,
And the blue vales a thousand joys recall,
See, to the last, last verge her infant steals!
O fly, yet stir not, speak not, lest it fall.
Far better taught, she lays her bosom bare,
And the fond boy springs back to nestle there.


## TO THE FRAGMENT OF A STATUE OF HERCULES, COMMONLY CALLED THE TORSO

And dost thou still, thou mass of breathing stone,
(Thy giant limbs to night and chaos hurl'd)
Still sit as on the fragment of a world;
Surviving all, majestic and alone?
What tho' the Spirits of the North, that swept
Rome from the earth, when in her pomp she slept,
Smote thee with fury, and thy headless trunk
Deep in the dust mid tower and temple sunk;
Soon to subdue mankind 'twas thine to rise.
Still, still unquell'd thy glorious energies!
Aspiring minds, with thee conversing, caught
Bright revelations of the Good they sought;
By thee that long-lost spell in secret given,
To draw down Gods, and lift the soul to Heav'n!


## TO —*

Ah! little thought she, when, with wild delight,
By many a torrent's shining track she flew,
When mountain-glens and caverns full of night
O'er her young mind divine enchantment threw,

That in her veins a secret horror slept,
That her light footsteps should be heard no more,
That she should die nor watch'd, alas, nor wept
By thee, unconscious of the pangs she bore.

Yet round her couch indulgent Fancy drew
The kindred, forms her closing eye requir'd.
There didst thou stand, there, with the smile she knew.
She mov'd her lips to bless thee, and expir'd.

And now to thee she comes; still, still the same
As in the hours gone unregarded by!
To thee, how chang'd, comes as she ever came;
Health on her cheek, and pleasure in her eye!

Nor less, less oft, as on that day, appears,
When lingering, as prophetic of the truth,
By the way-side she shed her parting tears
For ever lovely in the light of Youth?

*On the death of her sister.*

WRITTEN IN A SICK CHAMBER

There, in that bed so closely curtain'd round,
Worn to a shade, and wan with slow decay,
A father sleeps! Oh hush'd be every sound!
Soft may we breathe the midnight hours away!

He stirs, yet still he sleeps. May heavenly dreams
Long o'er his smooth and settled pillow rise;
Till thro' the shutter'd pane the morning streams,
And on the hearth the glimmering rush-light dies.

TO A FRIEND ON HIS MARRIAGE

On thee, blest youth, a father's hand confers
The maid thy earliest, fondest wishes knew.
Each soft enchantment of the soul is hers;
Thine be the joys to firm attachment due.

As on she moves with hesitating grace,
She wins assurance from his soothing voice;
And, with a look the pencil could not trace,
Smiles thro' her blushes, and confirms the choice.

Spare the fine tremors of her feeling frame!
To thee she turns, forgive a virgin's fears!
To thee she turns with surest, tenderest claim;
Weakness that charms, reluctance that endears!

At each response the sacred rite requires,
From her full bosom bursts the unbidden sigh.
A strange mysterious awe the scene inspires;
And on her lips the trembling accents die.

O'er her fair face what wild emotions play!
What lights and shades in sweet confusion blend!
Soon shall they fly, glad harbingers of day,
And settled sunshine on her soul descend!

Ah soon, thine own confest, ecstatic thought!
That hand shall strew thy summer-path with flowers;
And those blue eyes, with mildest lustre fraught,
Gild the calm current of domestic hours!


## THE ALPS AT DAY-BREAK

The sun-beams streak the azure skies,
And line with light the mountain's brow:
With hounds and horns the hunters rise,
And chase the roebuck thro' the snow.

From rock to rock, with giant-bound,
High on their iron poles they pass;
Mute, lest the air, convuls'd by sound,
Rend from above a frozen mass.

The goats wind slow their wonted way,
Up craggy steeps and ridges rude;
Mark'd by the wild wolf for his prey,
From desert cave or hanging wood.

And while the torrent thunders loud,
And as the echoing cliffs reply,
The huts peep o'er the morning-cloud,
Perch'd, like an eagle's nest, on high.


## IMITATION OF AN ITALIAN SONNET

Love, under Friendship's vesture white,
Laughs, his little limbs concealing;
And oft in sport, and oft in spite,
Like Pity meets the dazzled sight,
Smiles thro' his tears revealing.

But now as Rage the God appears!
He frowns, and tempests shake his frame!
Frowning, or smiling, or in tears,
'Tis Love; and Love is still the same.


## ON — ASLEEP

Sleep on, and dream of Heav'n awhile.
Tho' shut so close thy laughing eyes,
Thy rosy lips still seem to smile,

And move, and breathe delicious sighs!

Ah, now soft blushes tinge her cheeks,
And mantle o'er her neck of snow.
Ah, now she murmurs, now she speaks
What most I wish and fear to know.

She starts, she trembles, and she weeps!
Her fair hands folded on her breast.
And now, how like a saint she sleeps!
A seraph in the realms of rest!

Sleep on secure! Above controul,
Thy thoughts belong to Heav'n and thee!
And may the secret of thy soul
Repose within its sanctuary!


TO THE YOUNGEST DAUGHTER OF LADY —.

Ah! why with tell-tale tongue reveal
What most her blushes would conceal?
Why lift that modest veil to trace
The seraph-sweetness of her face?
Some fairer, better sport prefer;
And feel for us, if not for her.
For this presumption, soon or late,
Know thine shall be a kindred fate.
Another shall in vengeance rise
Sing Harriet's cheeks, and Harriet's eyes;
And, echoing back her wood-notes wild,
Trace all the mother in the child!


EPITAPH* ON A ROBIN REDBREAST

Tread lightly here, for here, 'tis said,
When piping winds are hush'd around,
A small note wakes from underground,
Where now his tiny bones are laid.
No more in lone and leafless groves,
With ruffled wing and faded breast,
His friendless, homeless spirit roves;
Gone to the world where birds are blest!
Where never cat glides o'er the green,
Or school-boy's giant form is seen;
But Love, and Joy, and smiling Spring
Inspire their little souls to sing!

## A WISH

Mine be a cot beside the hill,
A bee-hive's hum shall sooth my ear;
A willowy brook, that turns a mill,
With many a fall shall linger near.

The swallow, oft, beneath my thatch,
Shall twitter from her clay-built nest;
Oft shall the pilgrim lift the latch,
And share my meal, a welcome guest.

Around my ivy'd porch shall spring
Each fragrant flower that drinks the dew;
And Lucy, at her wheel, shall sing
In russet gown and apron blue.

The village-church, among the trees,
Where first our marriage-vows were giv'n,
With merry peals shall swell the breeze,
And point with taper spire to heav'n.

## AN ITALIAN SONG

Dear is my little native vale,
The ring-dove builds and murmurs there;
Close by my cot she tells her tale
To every passing villager.
The squirrel leaps from tree to tree,
And shells his nuts at liberty.

In orange-groves and myrtle-bowers,
That breathe a gale of fragrance round,
I charm the fairy-footed hours
With my lov'd lute's romantic sound;
Or crowns of living laurel weave,
For those that win the race at eve.

The shepherd's horn at break of day,
The ballet danc'd in twilight glade,
The canzonet and roundelay
Sung in the silent green-wood shade;
These simple joys, that never fail,
Shall bind me to my native vale.

## TO THE GNAT

When by the green-wood side, at summer eve,
Poetic visions charm my closing eye;
And fairy-scenes, that Fancy loves to weave,
Shift to wild notes of sweetest Minstrelsy;
'Tis thine to range in busy quest of prey,
Thy feathery antlers quivering with delight,
Brush from my lids the hues of heav'n away,
And all is Solitude, and all is Night!
Ah now thy barbed shaft, relentless fly,
Unsheaths its terrors in the sultry air!
No guardian sylph, in golden panoply,
Lifts the broad shield, and points the glittering spear.
Now near and nearer rush thy whirring wings,
Thy dragon-scales still wet with human gore.
Hark, thy shrill horn its fearful laram flings!
I wake in horror, and 'dare sleep no more!'

## AN INSCRIPTION

Shepherd, or Huntsman, or worn Mariner,
Whate'er thou art, who wouldst allay thy thirst,
Drink and be glad. This cistern of white stone,
Arch'd, and o'erwrought with many a sacred verse,
This iron cup chain'd for the general use,
And these rude seats of earth within the grove,
Were giv'n by FATIMA. Borne hence a bride,
'Twas here she turn'd from her beloved sire,
To see his face no more.  Oh, if thou canst,
('Tis not far off) visit his tomb with flowers;
And may some pious hand with water fill
The two small cells scoop'd in the marble there,
That birds may come and drink upon his grave,
Making it holy!

## CAPTIVITY

Caged in old woods, whose reverend echoes wake
When the hern screams along the distant lake,
Her little heart oft flutters to be free,
Oft sighs to turn the unrelenting key.
In vain! the nurse that rusted relic wears,
Nor mov'd by gold nor to be mov'd by tears;
And terraced walls their black reflection throw

On the green-mantled moat that sleeps below.


## A CHARACTER

As thro' the hedge-row shade the violet steals,
And the sweet air its modest leaf reveals;
Her softer charms, but by their influence known,
Surprise all hearts, and mould them to her own.


## WRITTEN IN THE HIGHLANDS OF SCOTLAND, SEPTEMBER 1, 1812

Blue was the loch, [*1] the clouds were gone,
Ben-Lomond in his glory shone,
When, Luss, I left thee; when the breeze
Bore me from thy silver sands,
Thy kirk-yard wall among the trees,
Where, grey with age, the dial stands;
That dial so well-known to me!
Tho' many a shadow it had shed,
Beloved Sister, since with thee
The legend on the stone was read.
The fairy-isles fled far away;
That with its woods and uplands green,
Where shepherd-huts are dimly seen,
And songs are heard at close of day;
That too, the deer's wild covert, fled,
And that, the Asylum of the Dead:
While, as the boat went merrily,
Much of ROB ROY [*2] the boat-man told;
His arm that fell below his knee,
His cattle-ford and mountain-hold.
Tarbet, [*3] thy shore I climb'd at last,
And, thy shady region pass'd,
Upon another shore I stood,
And look'd upon another flood; [*4]
Great Ocean's self! ('Tis He, who fills
That vast and awful depth of hills;)
Where many an elf was playing round,
Who treads unshod his classic ground;
And speaks, his native rocks among,
As FINGAL spoke, and OSSIAN sung.
Night fell; and dark and darker grew
That narrow sea, that narrow sky,
As o'er the glimmering waves we flew.
The sea-bird rustling, wailing by.
And now the grampus, half descried,
Black and huge above the tide;

The cliffs and promontories there,
Front to front, and broad and bare,
Each beyond each, with giant-feet
Advancing as in haste to meet;
The shatter'd fortress, whence the Dane
Blew his shrill blast, nor rush'd in vain,
Tyrant of the drear domain;
All into midnight-shadow sweep
When day springs upward from the deep! [*5]
Kindling the waters in its flight,
The prow wakes splendour; and the oar,
That rose and fell unseen before,
Flashes in a sea of light!
Glad sign, and sure! for now we hail
Thy flowers, Glenfinart, in the gale;
And bright indeed the path should be,
That leads to Friendship and to Thee!
Oh blest retreat, and sacred too!
Sacred as when the bell of prayer
Toll'd duly on the desert air,
And crosses deck'd thy summits blue.
Oft, like some lov'd romantic tale,
Oft shall my weary mind recall,
Amid the hum and stir of men,
Thy beechen grove and waterfall,
Thy ferry with its gliding sail,
And Her the Lady of the Glen!

*1: Loch-Lomond.
*2: A famous out-law.
*3: Signifying in the Erse language an Isthmus.
*4: Loch-Long.
*5: A phenomenon described by many navigators.


A FAREWELL

Once more, enchanting girl, adieu!
I must be gone while yet I may,
Oft shall I weep to think of you;
But here I will not, cannot stay.

The sweet expression of that face.
For ever changing, yet the same,
Ah no, I dare not turn to trace.
It melts my soul, it fires my frame!

Yet give me, give me, ere I go,
One little lock of those so blest,
That lend your cheek a warmer glow,

And on your white neck love to rest.

Say, when to kindle soft delight,
That hand has chanc'd with mine to meet,
How could its thrilling touch excite
A sigh so short, and yet so sweet?

O say but no, it must not be.
Adieu! A long, a long adieu!
Yet still, methinks, you frown on me;
Or never could I fly from you.

Child of the sun! pursue thy rapturous flight,
Mingling with her thou lov'st in fields of light;
And, where the flowers of paradise unfold,
Quaff fragrant nectar from their cups of gold.
There shall thy wings, rich as an evening-sky,
Expand and shut with silent ecstasy!
Yet wert thou once a worm, a thing that crept
On the bare earth, then wrought a tomb and slept!
And such is man; soon from his cell of clay
To burst a seraph in the blaze of day!


VERSES WRITTEN IN WESTMINSTER ABBEY

Whoe'er thou art, approach, and, with a sigh,
Mark where the small remains of Greatness lie.
There sleeps the dust of Him for ever gone;
How near the Scene where once his Glory shone!
And, tho' no more ascends the voice of Prayer,
Tho' the last footsteps cease to linger there,
Still, like an awful Dream that comes again,
Alas, at best, as transient and as vain,
Still do I see (while thro' the vaults of night
The funeral-song once more proclaims the rite)
The moving Pomp along the shadowy Isle,
That, like a Darkness, fill'd the solemn Pile;
The illustrious line, that in long order led,
Of those that lov'd Him living, mourn'd Him dead;
Of those, the Few, that for their Country stood
Round Him who dar'd be singularly good;
All, of all ranks, that claim'd Him for their own;
And nothing wanting but Himself alone!
Oh say, of Him now rests there but a name;
Wont, as He was, to breathe ethereal flame?

Friend of the Absent! Guardian of the Dead!
Who but would here their sacred sorrows shed?
(Such as He shed on NELSON'S closing grave;
How soon to claim the sympathy He gave!)
In Him, resentful of another's wrong,
The dumb were eloquent, the feeble strong.
Truth from his lips a charm celestial drew
Ah, who so mighty and so gentle too?
What tho' with War the madding Nations rung,
'Peace,' when He spoke, dwelt ever on his tongue!
Amidst the frowns of Power, the tricks of State,
Fearless, resolv'd, and negligently great!
In vain malignant vapours gather'd round;
He walk'd, erect, on consecrated ground.
The clouds, that rise to quench the Orb of day,
Reflect its splendour, and dissolve away!
When in retreat He laid his thunder by,
For letter'd ease and calm Philosophy,
Blest were his hours within the silent grove,
Where still his god-like Spirit deigns to rove;
Blest by the orphan's smile, the widow's prayer,
For many a deed, long done in secret there.
There shone his lamp on Homer's hallow'd page.
There, listening, sate the hero and the sage;
And they, by virtue and by blood allied,
Whom most He lov'd, and in whose arms He died.
Friend of all Human-kind! not here alone
(The voice, that speaks, was not to Thee unknown)
Wilt Thou be miss'd, O'er every land and sea
Long, long shall England be rever'd in Thee!
And, when the Storm is hush'd in distant years
Foes on thy grave shall meet, and mingle tears!


THE VOYAGE OF COLUMBUS

*CHI SE' TU, CHE VIENI -?*
*DA ME STESSO NON VEGNO.*
*DANTE*

*I have seen the day,*
*That I have worn a visor, and could tell*
*A tale*
*SHAKSPEARE.*


PREFACE

The following Poem (or, to speak more properly, what remains of it* has here and there a lyrical turn of thought and expression. It is sudden in its transitions, and full of historical allusions; leaving much to be imagined by the reader.

The subject is a voyage the most memorable in the annals of mankind. Columbus was a person of extraordinary virtue and piety, acting under the sense of a divine impulse; and his achievement the discovery of a New World, the inhabitants of which were shut out from the light of Revelation, and given up, as they believed, to the dominion of malignant spirits.

Many of the incidents will now be thought extravagant; yet they were once perhaps received with something more than indulgence. It was an age of miracles; and who can say that among the venerable legends in the library of the Escurial, or the more authentic records which fill the great chamber in the Archivo of Simancas, and which relate entirely to the deep tragedy of America, there are no volumes that mention the marvellous things here described? Indeed the story, as already told throughout Europe, admits of no heightening. Such was the religious enthusiasm of the early writers, that the Author had only to transfuse it into his verse; and he appears to have done little more; though some of the circumstances, which he alludes to as well-known, have long ceased to be so. By using the language of that day, he has called up Columbus 'in his habit as he lived;' and the authorities, such as exist, are carefully given by the translator.

*The Original in the Castilian language, according to the Inscription that fellows, was found among other MSS. in an old religious house near Palos, situated on an island formed by the river Tinto, and dedicated to our Lady of Rábida. The Writer describes himself as having sailed with Columbus; but his style and manner are evidently of an after-time.

INSCRIBED ON THE ORIGINAL MANUSCRIPT

Unclasp me, Stranger; and unfold,
With trembling care, my leaves of gold
Rich in gothic portraiture
If yet, alas, a leaf endure.
In RABIDA'S monastic fane
I cannot ask, and ask in vain.
The language of CASTILE I speak;
Mid many an Arab, many a Greek,
Old in the days of CHARLEMAIN;
When minstrel-music wander' round,
And Science, waking, bless' the sound.
No earthly thought has here a place;
The cowl let down on every face.
Yet here, in consecrated dust,
Here would I sleep, if sleep I must.
From GENOA when COLUMBUS came,
(At once her glory and her shame)
'Was here he caught the holy flame.
'Twas here the generous vow he made;
His banners on the altar laid.
One hallow'd morn, methought,
I felt As if a soul within me dwelt!
But who arose and gave to me

The sacred trust I keep for thee,
And in his cell at even-tide
Knelt before the cross and died
Inquire not now. His name no more
Glimmers on the chancel-floor,
Near the lights that ever shine
Before ST. MARY'S blessed shrine.
To me one little hour devote,
And lay thy staff and scrip beside thee;
Read in the temper that he wrote,
And may his gentle spirit guide thee!
My leaves forsake me, one by one;
The book-worm thro' and thro' has gone.
Oh haste, unclasp me, and unfold;
The tale within was never told!


THE ARGUMENT

Columbus, having wandered from kingdom to kingdom, at length obtains three ships and sets sail on the Atlantic. The compass alters from its antient direction; the wind becomes constant and unremitting; night and day he advances, till he is suddenly stopped in his course by a mass of vegetation, extending as far as the eye can reach, and assuming the appearance of a country overwhelmed by the sea. Alarm and despondence on board. He resigns himself to the care of Heaven, and proceeds on his voyage; while columns of water move along in his path before him.

Meanwhile the deities of America assemble in council; and one of the Zemi, the gods of the islanders, announces his approach. "In vain," says he, "have we guarded the Atlantic for ages. A mortal has baffled our power; nor will our votaries arm against him. Yours are a sterner race. Hence; and, while we have recourse to stratagem, do you array the nations round your altars, and prepare for an exterminating war." They disperse while he is yet speaking; and, in the shape of a condor, he directs his flight to the fleet. His journey described. He arrives there. A panic. A mutiny. Columbus restores order; continues on his voyage; and lands in a New World. Ceremonies of the first interview. Rites of hospitality. The ghost of Cazziva.

Two months pass away, and an Angel, appearing in a dream to Columbus, thus addresses him: "Return to Europe; though your Adversaries, such is the will of Heaven, shall let loose the hurricane against you. A little while shall they triumph; insinuating themselves into the hearts of your followers, and making the World, which you came to bless, a scene of blood and slaughter. Yet is there cause for rejoicing. Your work is done. The cross of Christ is planted here; and, in due time, all things shall be made perfect!"


CANTO I

**Night - Columbus on the Atlantic - the variation of the compass, &c.**

Say who first pass'd the portals of the West,
And the great Secret of the Deep possess'd;
Who first the standard of his Faith unfurl'd
On the dread confines of an unknown World;

Sung ere his coming and by Heav'n design'd
To lift the veil that cover'd half mankind!
'Twas night. The Moon, o'er the wide wave, disclos'd
Her awful face; and Nature's self repos'd;
When, slowly rising in the azure sky,
Three white sails shone but to no mortal eye.
Entering a boundless sea. In slumber cast,
The very ship-boy, on the dizzy mast,
Half breath'd his orisons! Alone unchang'd,
Calmly, beneath, the great Commander rang'd,
Thoughtful not sad; and, as the planet grew,
His noble form, wrapt in his mantle blue,
Athwart the deck a solemn shadow threw.
"Thee hath it pleas'd. Thy will be done!" he said,
Then sought his cabin; and, their capas* spread,
Around him lay the sleeping as the dead,
When, by his lamp, to that mysterious Guide,
On whose still counsels all his hopes relied,
That Oracle to man in mercy giv'n,
Whose voice is truth, whose wisdom is from heav'n,
Who over sands and seas directs the stray,
And, as with God's own finger, points the way,
He turn'd; but what strange thoughts perplex'd his soul,
When, lo, no more attracted to the Pole,
The Compass, faithless as the circling vane,
Flutter'd and fix'd, flutter'd and fix'd again;
And still, as by some unseen Hand imprest,
Explor'd, with trembling energy, the West!
"Ah no!" he cried, and calm'd his anxious brow.
"Ill, nor the signs of ill, 'tis thine to show.
Thine but to lead me where I wish'd to go!"
COLUMBUS err'd not.  In that awful hour,
Sent forth to save, and girt with God-like power,
And glorious as the regent of the sun,
An Angel came! He spoke, and it was done!
He spoke, and, at his call, a mighty Wind,
Not like the fitful blast, with fury blind,
But deep, majestic, in its destin'd course,
Rush'd with unerring, unrelenting force,
From the bright East. Tides duly ebb'd and flow'd;
Stars rose and set; and new horizons glow'd;
Yet still it blew! As with primeval sway,
Still did its ample spirit, night and day,
Move on the waters! All, resign'd to Fate,
Folded their arms and sat; and seem'd to wait
Some sudden change; and sought, in chill suspense,
New spheres of being, and new modes of sense;
As men departing, tho' not doom'd to die,
And midway on their passage to eternity.

*1: The capa is the Spanish cloak.

**The Voyage continued.**

"What vast foundations in the Abyss are there,
As of a former world? Is it not where
ATLANTIC kings their barbarous pomp display'd;
Sunk into darkness with the realms they sway'd,
When towers and temples, thro' the closing wave,
A glimmering ray of antient splendour gave
And we shall rest with them. Arise, behold,

We stop to stir no more...nor will the tale be told."
The pilot smote his breast; the watch-man cried
"Land!" and his voice in faltering accents died.
At once the fury of the prow was quell'd;
And (whence or why from many an age withheld)
Shrieks, not of men, were mingling in the blast;
And armed shapes of god-like stature pass'd!
Slowly along the evening sky they went,
As on the edge of some vast battlement;
Helmet and shield, and spear and gonfalon
Streaming a baleful light that was not of the sun!

Long from the stern the great Adventurer gaz'd
With awe not fear; then high his hands he rais'd.
"Thou All-supreme - in goodness as in power,
Who, from his birth to this eventful hour,
Hast led thy servant over land and sea,
Confessing Thee in all, and all in Thee,
Oh still" He spoke, and lo, the charm accurst
Fled whence it came, and the broad barrier burst!
A vain illusion! (such as mocks the eyes
Of fearful men, when mountains round them rise
From less than nothing nothing now beheld,
But scatter'd sedge, repelling, and repell'd!
And once again that valiant company
Right onward came, ploughing the Unknown Sea.
Already borne beyond the range of thought,
With Light divine, with Truth immortal fraught,
From world to world their steady course they keep,
Swift as the winds along the waters sweep,
Mid the mute nations of the purple deep.
And now the sound of harpy-wings they hear;
Now less and less, as vanishing in fear!
And, see, the heav'ns bow down, the waters rise.
And, rising, shoot in columns to the skies,
That stand and still, when they proceed, retire,

As in the Desert burn'd the sacred fire;
Moving in silent majesty, till Night
Descends, and shuts the vision from their sight.

**An Assembly of Evil Spirits.**

Tho' chang'd my cloth of gold for amice grey
In my spring-time, when every month was May,
With hawk and hound I cours'd away the hour,
Or sung my roundelay in lady's bower.
And tho' my world be now a narrow cell,
(Renounc'd for ever all I lov'd so well)
Tho' now my head be bald, my feet be bare,
And scarce my knees sustain my book of prayer,
Oh I was there, one of that gallant crew,
And saw and wonder'd whence his Power He drew,
Yet little thought, tho' by his side I stood,
Of his great Foes in earth and air and flood,
Then uninstructed. But my sand is run,
And the Night coming - and my Task not done!
'Twas in the deep, immeasurable cave
Of ANDES, echoing to the Southern wave,
Mid pillars of Basalt, the work of fire,
That, giant-like, to upper day aspire,
'Twas there that now, as wont in heav'n to shine,
Forms of angelic mould, and grace divine,
Assembled. All, exil'd the realms of rest,
In vain the sadness of their souls suppress'd;
Yet of their glory many a scatter'd ray
Shot thro' the gathering shadows of decay.
Each mov'd a God; and all, as Gods, possess'd
One half the globe; from pole to pole confess'd!
These in dim shrines and barbarous symbols reign,
Where PLATA and MARAGNON meet the Main.
Those the wild hunter worships as he roves,
In the green shade of CHILI'S fragrant groves;
Or warrior-tribes with rites of blood implore,
Whose night-fires gleam along the sullen shore
Of HURON or ONTARIO, inland seas,
What time the song of death is in the breeze!
'Twas now in dismal pomp and order due,
While the vast concave flash'd with lightnings blue,
On shining pavements of metallic ore,
That many an age the fusing sulphur bore,
They held high council. All was silence round,
When, with a voice most sweet yet most profound,
A sovereign Spirit burst the gates of night,

And from his wings of gold shook drops of liquid light!
MERION, commission'd with his host to sweep
From age to age the melancholy deep!
Chief of the ZEMI, whom the Isles obey'd,
By Ocean sever'd from a world of shade.


I.

"Prepare, again prepare,"
Thus o'er the soul the thrilling accents' came,
"Thrones to resign for lakes of living flame,
And triumph for despair.
He, on whose call afflicting thunders wait,
Has will'd it; and his will is fate!
In vain the legions, emulous to save,
Hung in the tempest o'er the troubled main;
Turn'd each presumptuous prow that broke the wave,
And dash'd it on its shores again.
All is fulfill'd! Behold, in close array,
What mighty banners stream in the bright track of day!"


II.

"No voice, as erst, shall in the desert rise;
Nor antient, dread solemnities
With scorn of death the trembling tribes inspire.
Wreaths for the Conqueror's brow the victims bind!
Yet, tho' we fled yon firmament of fire,
Still shall we fly, all hope of rule resign'd?"

He' spoke; and all was silence, all was night!
Each had already wing'd his formidable flight.


CANTO IV

**The Voyage continued.**

"Ah, why look back, tho' all is left behind?
No sounds of life are stirring in the wind.
And you, ye birds, winging your passage home,
How blest ye are! We know not where we roam,
We go," they cried, "go to return no more;
Nor ours, alas, the transport to explore
A human footstep on a desert shore!"

Still, as beyond this mortal life impell'd
By some mysterious energy, He held
His everlasting course. Still self-possess'd,
High on the deck He stood, disdaining rest;

(His amber chain the only badge he bore,
His mantle blue such as his fathers wore)
Fathom'd, with searching hand, the dark profound,
And scatter'd hope and glad assurance round.
At day-break might the Caravels* be seen,
Chasing their shadows o'er the deep serene;
Their burnish'd prows lash'd by the sparkling tide.
Their green-cross standards waving far and wide.
And now once more to better thoughts inclin'd,
The sea-man, mounting, clamour'd in the wind.
The soldier told his tales of love and war;
The courtier sung, sung to his gay guitar.
Round, at Primero, sate a whisker'd band;
So Fortune smil'd, careless of sea or land!
LEON, MONTALVAN, (serving side by side;
Two with one soul and, as they liv'd, they died)
VASCO the brave, thrice found among the slain,
Thrice, and how soon, up and in arms again,
As soon to wish he had been sought in vain,
Chain'd down in Fez, beneath the bitter thong,
To the hard bench and heavy oar so long!
ALBERT of FLORENCE, who, at twilight-time,
In my young ear pour'd DANTE'S tragic rhyme,
Screen'd by the sail as near the mast we lay,
Our night illumin'd by the ocean-spray;
LERMA "the generous", AVILA "the proud;"
VELASQUEZ, GARCIA, thro' the echoing croud
Trac'd by their mirth from EBRO'S classic shore,
From golden TAJO to return no more!

*Light vessels, formerly used by the Spaniards and Portuguese.


CANTO V

**The Voyage continued**

Yet who but He undaunted could explore
A world of waves a sea without a shore,
Trackless and vast and wild as that reveal'd
When round the Ark the birds of tempest wheel'd;
When all was still in the destroying hour
No sign of man! no vestige of his power!
One at the stern before the hour-glass stood,
As 'twere to count the sands; one o'er the flood
Gaz'd for St. Elmo; [1*] while another cried
"Once more good morrow!" and sate down and sigh'd.
Day, when it came, came only with its light.
Tho' long invok'd, 'twas sadder than the night!
Look where He would, for ever as He turn'd,

He met the eye of one that inly mourn'd.
Then sunk his generous spirit, and He wept.
The friend, the father rose; the hero slept.
PALOS, thy port, with many a pang resign' d,
Fill'd with its busy scenes his lonely mind;
The solemn march, the vows in concert giv'n, [*2]
The bended knees and lifted hands to heav'n,
The incens'd rites, and choral harmonies,
The Guardian's blessings mingling with his sighs;
While his dear boys, ah, on his neck they hung,
And long at parting to his garments clung.
Oft in the silent night-watch doubt and fear
Broke in uncertain murmurs on his ear.
Oft the stern Catalan, at noon of day,
Mutter'd dark threats, and linger'd to obey;
Tho' that brave Youth, he, whom his courser bore
Right thro' the midst, when, fetlock deep in gore,
The great GONZALO [*3] battled with the Moor,
(What time the ALHAMBRA shook, soon to unfold
Its sacred courts, and fountains yet untold,
Its holy texts and arabesques of gold)
Tho' ROLDAN, [*4] sleep and death to him alike,
Grasp'd his good sword and half unsheath'd to strike.
"Oh born to wander with your flocks," he cried,
"And bask and dream along the mountain-side;
To urge your mules, tinkling from hill to hill;
Or at the vintage-feast to drink your fill,
And strike your castanets, with gipsy-maid
Dancing Fandangos in the chesnut shade
Come on," he cried, and threw his glove in scorn,
"Not this your wonted pledge, the brimming horn.
Valiant in peace! Adventurous at home!
Oh, had ye vow'd with pilgrim-staff to roam;
Or with banditti sought the sheltering wood,
Where mouldering crosses mark the scene of blood!"
He said, he drew; then, at his Master's frown,
Sullenly sheath'd, plunging the weapon down.

*1: A luminous appearance of good omen.
*2: His public procession to the Convent of Rábida on the day before he set sail. It was there that his sons had received their education; and he himself appears to have passed some time there, the venerable Guardian, Juan Perez de Marchena, being his zealous and affectionate friend. The ceremonies of his departure and return are represented in many of the fresco-paintings in the palaces of Genoa.
*3: Gonzalo Fernandez, already known by the name of The great Captain. Granada surrendered on the 2nd of January, 1492. Columbus set sail on the, 3rd of August following.
*4: Probably a soldier of fortune. There were more than one of the name on board.

## The Flight of an Angel of Darkness

War and the Great in War let others sing.
Havoc and spoil, and tears and triumphing;
The morning-march that flashes to the sun,
The feast of vultures when the day is done;
And the strange tale of many slain for one!
I sing a Man, amidst his sufferings here,
Who watch'd and serv'd in humbleness and fear;
Gentle to others, to himself severe.

Still unsubdued by Danger's varying form,
Still, as unconscious of the coming storm,
He look'd elate! His beard, his mien sublime,
Shadow'd by Age; by Age before the time,
From many a sorrow borne in many a clime,
Mov'd every heart. And now in opener skies
Stars yet unnam'd of purer radiance rise!
Stars, milder suns, that love a shade to cast,
And on the bright wave fling the trembling mast. [* 1]

'Twas the mid hour, when He, whose accents dread
Still wander'd thro' the regions of the dead,
(MERION, commission'd with his host to sweep
From age to age the melancholy deep)
To elude the seraph-guard that watch'd for man,
And mar, as erst, the Eternal's perfect plan,
Rose like the Condor, and, at towering height,
In pomp of plumage sail'd, deepening the shades of night.
Roc of the West! to him all empire giv'n!
Who bears [*2] Axalhua's dragon-folds to heav'n; [*3]
His flight a whirlwind, and, when heard afar,
Like thunder, or the distant din of war!
Mountains and seas fled backward as he pass'd
O'er the great globe, by not a cloud o'ercast
From the ANTARCTICK, from the Land of Fire [*4]
To where ALASKA'S [*5] wintry wilds retire;
From mines [*6] of gold, and giant-sons of earth,
To grotts of ice, and tribes of pigmy birth
Who freeze alive, nor, dead, in dust repose,
High-hung in forests to the casing snows.
Now mid angelic multitudes he flies,
That hourly come with blessings from the skies;
Wings the blue element, and, borne sublime,
Eyes the set sun, gilding each distant clime;
Then, like a meteor, shooting to the main,
Melts into pure intelligence again.

*1: Splendour of the nights in a tropical climate.
*2: Axalhua, or the Emperor. The name in the Mexican language for the great serpent of America.

*3: As the Roc of the East is said to have carried off the Elephant. See Marco Polo.
*4: Tierra del Fuego.
*5: Northern extremity of the New World. See Cook's last Voyage.
*6: Mines of Chili; which extend, says Ovalle, to the Strait of Magellan. I. 4.


## CANTO VII

### A Mutiny Excited

What tho' Despondence reign'd, and wild Affright;
Stretch'd in the midst, and, thro' that dismal night,
By his white plume reveal'd and buskins white,
Slept ROLDAN. When he clos'd his gay career,
Hope fled for ever, and with Hope fled Fear,
Blest with each gift indulgent Fortune sends,
Birth and its rights, wealth and its train of friends,
Star-like he shone! Now beggar'd, and alone,
Danger he woo'd, and claim'd her for his own.
O'er him a Vampire [*1] his dark wings display'd.
'Twas MERION'S self, covering with dreadful shade.
He came, and, couch'd on ROLDAN'S ample breast,
Each secret pore of breathing life possess'd,
Fanning the sleep that seem'd his final rest;
Then, inly gliding like a subtle flame,
Subdued the man, and from his thrilling frame
Sent forth the voice! "We live, we breathe no more!
The fatal wind blows on the dreary shore!
On yonder cliffs, beckoning their fellow-prey,
The spectres stalk, and murmur at delay!
Yet if thou canst (not for myself I plead,
Mine but to follow where 'tis thine to lead)
Oh turn and save! To thee, with streaming eyes,
To thee each widow kneels, each orphan cries!
Who now, condemn'd the lingering hours to tell,
Think and but think of those they lov'd so well!"
All melt in tears! but what can tears avail?
These climb the mast, and shift the swelling sail.
These snatch the helm; and round me now I hear
Smiting of hands, out-cries of grief and fear,
(That In the aisles at midnight haunt me still,
Turning my lonely thoughts from good to ill)
"Were there no graves, none in our land," they cry,
"That thou hast brought us on the deep to die?"
Silent with sorrow, long within his cloak
His face He muffled, then the Hero spoke.
"Generous and brave! when God himself is' here,
Why shake at shadows in your mid career?
He can suspend the Jaws himself design'd,
He walks the waters, and the winged wind;

Himself your guide! and yours the high behest
To lift your voice, and bid a world be blest!
And can you shrink? [*2] to you, to you consign'd
The glorious privilege to serve mankind!
Oh had I perish'd, when my failing frame [*3]
Clung to the shatter'd oar mid wrecks of flame!
Was it for this I linger'd life away,
The scorn of Folly, and of Fraud the prey;
Bow'd down my mind, the gift His bounty gave,
At courts a suitor, and to slaves a slave?
Yet in His name whom only we should fear,
('Tis all, all I shall ask, or you shall hear)
Grant but three days" He spoke not uninspir'd; [*4]
And each in silence to his watch retir'd.
At length among us came an unknown Voice!
"Go, if ye will; and, if ye can, rejoice.
Go, with unbidden guests the banquet share.
In his own shape shall Death receive you there." [*5]

*1: A species of bat in S. America; which refreshes by the gentle agitation of its wings, while it sucks
the blood of the sleeper, turning his sleep into death. Ulloa.
*2: The same language had been addressed to Isabella. F..Cpl. c 15.
*3: His miraculous escape, in early life, during a sea-fight off the coast of Portugal.
*4: He used to affirm, that he stood in need of God's particular assistance; like Moses, when he led
forth the people of Israel, who forbore to lay violent hands upon him, because of the miracles which
God wrought by his means. 'So,' said the Admiral, 'did it happen to me on that voyage.' F. Columbus,
c. 19. 'And so easily,' says a Commentator, 'are the workings of the Evil one
overcome by the power of God!'
*5: This denunciation, fulfilled as it appears to be in the eleventh canto, may remind the reader of the
Harpy's in Virgil. Æn. III v. 247.


CANTO VIII

**Land Discovered**

Twice in the zenith blaz'd the orb of light;
No shade, all sun, insufferably bright!
Then the long line found rest [*1] in coral groves
Silent and dark, where the sea-lion roves:
And all on deck, kindling to life again,
Sent forth their anxious spirits o'er the main.
"Oh whence, as wafted from Elysium, whence
These perfumes, strangers to the raptur'd sense?
These boughs of gold, and fruits of heav'nly hue,
Tinging with vermeil light the billows blue?
And (thrice, thrice blessed is the eye that spied,
The hand that snatch'd it sparkling in the tide)
Whose cunning carv'd this vegetable bowl,
Symbol of social rites, and intercourse of soul?"

Such to their grateful ear the gush of springs,
Who course the ostrich, as away she wings;
Sons of the desert! who delight to dwell
Mid kneeling camels round the sacred well.
The sails were furl'd: [*2] with many a melting close,
Solemn and slow the evening anthem rose,
Rose to the Virgin. 'Twas the hour of day,
When setting suns o'er summer-seas display
A path of glory, opening in the west
To golden climes, and islands of the blest;
And human voices, on the silent air,
Went o'er the waves in songs of gladness there!
Chosen of Men! 'twas thine, at noon of night,
First from the prow to hail the glimmering light; [*3]
(Emblem of Truth divine, whose secret ray
Enters the soul, and makes the darkness day!)
"PEDRO! RODRIGO! [*4] there, methought, it shone!
There, in the west! and now, alas, 'tis gone!
'Twas all a dream! we gaze and gaze in vain!
But mark and speak not, there it comes again!
It moves! what form unseen, what being there
With torch-like lustre fires the murky air?
His instincts, passions, say, how like our own?
Oh! when will day reveal a world unknown?"

*1: For thirty-five days they were advancing 'where fathom-line could never touch the ground.'
*2: On Thursday, the 11th of October, 1492.
*3: A light in the midst of darkness, signifying the spiritual light that he came to spread there. F. Col. c. 22. Herrera, I i 12.
*4: Pedro Gutierrez, a Page of the King's Chamber. Rodrigo Sanchez of Segovia, Comptroller of the Fleet.


CANTO IX

**The New World**

Long on the wave the morning mists repos'd,
Then broke and, melting into light, disclos'd
Half-circling hills, whose everlasting woods
Sweep with their sable skirts the shadowy floods.
And say, when all, to holy transport giv'n,
Embraced and wept as at the gates of Heav'nly,
When one and all of us, repentant, ran,
And, on our faces, bless' the wondrous Man;
Say, was I then deceiv'd, or from the skies
Burst on my ear seraphic harmonies?
"Glory to God!" unnumber'd voices sung,
"Glory to God!" the vales and mountains rung,
Voices that hail' Creation's primal morn,

And to the shepherds sung a Saviour born.
Slowly to land the sacred cross we bore,
And, kneeling, kiss'd with pious lips the shore.
But how the scene pour tray?] Nymphs of romance,
Youths graceful as the Faun, with rapturous glance,
Spring from the glades, and down the green steeps run,
To greet their mighty guests, "The children of the Sun!"
Features so fair, in garments richly wrought,
From citadels, with Heav'n's own thunder fraught,
Check'd their light footsteps, statue-like they stood,
As worshipp'd forms, the Genii of the Wood!
But see, the regal plumes, the couch of state!
Still, where it moves, the wise in council wait!
See now borne forth the monstrous mask of gold,
And ebon chair of many a serpent-fold;
These now exchang'd for gifts that thrice surpass
The wondrous ring, and lamp, and horse of brass.
What long-drawn tube transports the gazer home,
Kindling with stars at noon the ethereal dome?
'Tis here: and here circles of solid light
Charm with another self the cheated sight;
As man to man another self disclose,
That now with terror starts, with triumph glows!


CANTO X

### Cora - Luxuriant Vegetation - the Humming-Bird - the Fountain of Youth

Then CORA came, the youngest of her race,
And in her hands she hid her lovely face;
Yet oft by stealth a timid glance she cast,
And now with playful step the Mirror pass'd,
Each bright reflection brighter than the last!
And oft behind it flew, and oft before;
The more she search'd, pleas'd and perplex'd the more!
And look'd and laugh'd, and blush'd with quick surprize;
Her lips all mirth, all ecstasy her eyes!
But soon the telescope attracts her view;
And lo, her lover in his light canoe
Rocking, at noon-tide, on the silent sea,
Before her lies!  It cannot, cannot be.
Late as he left the shore, she linger'd there,
Till, less and less, he melted into air!
Sigh after sigh steals from her gentle frame,
And say, that murmur, was it not his name?
She turns, and thinks; and, lost in wild amaze,
Gazes again, and could for ever gaze!
Nor can thy flute, ALONSO, now excite,
As in VALENCIA, when, with fond delight,

FRANCISCA, waking, to the lattice flew,
So soon to love and to be wretched too!
Hers thro' a convent-grate to send her last adieu.
Yet who now comes uncall'd; and round and round,
And near and nearer flutters to its sound;
Then stirs not, breathes not on enchanted ground?
Who now lets fall the flowers she cull'd to wear
When he, who promis'd, should at eve be there;
And faintly smiles, and hangs her head aside
The tear that glistens on her cheek to hide?
Ah, who but CORA? till inspir'd, possess'd,
At once she springs, and clasps it to her breast!

Soon from the bay the mingling croud ascends,
Kindred first met! by sacred instinct Friends!
Thro' citron groves, and fields of yellow maize,
Thro' plantain-walks where not a sun-beam plays.
Here blue savannas fade into the sky.
There forests frown in midnight majesty;
Ceiba, and Indian fig, and plane sublime,
Nature's first-born, and reverenc'd by Time!
There sits the bird that speaks! [*1] there, quivering, rise
Wings that reflect the glow of evening skies!
Half bird, half fly, the fairy king of flowers [*2]
Reigns there, and revels thro' the fragrant hours;
Gem full of life, and joy, and song divine,
Soon in the virgin's graceful ear to shine.
'Twas he that sung, if antient Fame speaks truth,
"Come! follow, follow to the Fount of Youth!
I quaff the ambrosial mists that round it rise,
Dissolv'd and lost in dreams of Paradise!"
For there call'd forth, to bless a happier hour,
It met the sun in many a rainbow-shower!
Murmuring delight, its living waters roll'd
'Mid branching palms and amaranths of gold! [*3]

*1: The Parrot, as described by Aristotle. Hist. Animal, viii. 12.
*2: The Humming-bird. Kakopit (florum regulus) is the name of an Indian bird, referred to this class
by Seba.
*3: According to an antient tradition. See Oviedo, Vega, Herrera, &c. Not many years afterwards a
Spaniard of distinction wandered every where in search of it; and no wonder, as Robertson observes,
when Columbus himself could imagine that he had found the seat of Paradise,

CANTO XI

**Evening, a Banquet, the Ghost of Cazziva.**

Her leaves at length the conscious tamarind clos'd,
And from wild sport the marmoset repos'd;

Fresh from the lake the breeze of twilight blew,
And vast and deep the mountain-shadows grew;
When many a fire-fly, shooting thro' the glade,
Spangled the locks of many a lovely maid,
Who now danc'd forth to strew His path with flowers.
And hymn His welcome to celestial bowers.
There od'rous lamps adorn'd the festal rite,
And guavas blush'd as in the vales of light, [*1]
There silent sat many an unbidden Guest, [*2]
Whose stedfast looks a secret dread impress'd;
Not there forgot the sacred fruit that fed
At nightly feasts the Spirits of the Dead,
Mingling in scenes that mirth to mortals give,
Tho' by their sadness known from those that live.
There met, as erst, within the wonted grove,
Unmarried girls and youths that died for love!
Sons now beheld their antient sires again;
And sires, alas, their sons in battle slain!
But whence that sigh? 'Twas from a heart that broke!
And whence that voice? As from the grave it spoke!
And who, as unresolv'd the feast to share,
Sits half-withdrawn in faded splendour there?
'Tis he of yore, the warrior and the sage,
Whose lips have mov'd in prayer from age to age;
Whose eyes, that wander'd as in search before,
Now on COLUMBUS fix'd, to search no more!
CAZZIVA, [*3] gifted in his day to know
The gathering signs of a long night of woe;
Gifted by Those who give but to enslave;
No rest in death! no refuge in the grave!
With sudden spring as at the shout of war,
He flies! and, turning in his flight, from far
Glares thro' the gloom like some portentous star!
Unseen, unheard! Hence, Minister of Ill! [*4]
Hence, 'tis not yet the hour; tho' come it will!
They that foretold, too soon shall they fulfil; [*5]
When forth they rush as with the torrent's sweep, [*6]
And deeds are done that make the Angels weep!

Hark, o'er the busy mead the shell proclaim
Triumphs, and masques, and high heroic games.
And now the old sit round; and now the young
Climb the green boughs, the murmuring doves among.
Who claims the prize, when winged feet contend;
When twanging bows the flaming arrows send?
Who stands self-centred in the field of fame,
And, grappling, flings to earth a giant's frame?
Whilst all, with anxious hearts and eager eyes,
Bend as he bends, and, as he rises, rise!
And CORA'S self, in pride of beauty here,
Trembles with grief and joy, and hope and fear!

(She who, the fairest, ever flew the first,
With cup of balm to quench his burning thirst;
Knelt at his head, her fan-leaf in her hand,
And humm'd the air that pleas'd him, while she fann'd)
How blest his lot! tho', by the Muse unsung,
His name shall perish, when his knell is rung.

That night, transported, with a sigh I said
"'Tis all a dream!" Now, like a dream, 'tis fled;
And many and many a year has pass'd away,
And I alone remain to watch and pray!
Yet oft in darkness, on my bed of straw,
Oft I awake and think on what I saw!
The groves, the birds, the youths, the nymphs recall,
And CORA, loveliest, sweetest of them all!

*1: They believed that the souls of good men were conveyed to a pleasant valley, abounding in guavas and other delicious fruits. Herrera, I. iii. 3. F Columbus, c. 62.
*2: "The dead walk abroad in the night, and feast with the living;" (F. Columbus, c. 62) and "eat of the fruit called Guannàba." P. Martyr, dec. I. 9.
*3: An antient Cacique, in his life-time and after his death, employed by the Zemi to alarm his people. See F. Columbus, c. 62.
*4: The Author is speaking in his inspired character. Hidden things arc revealed to him, and placed before his mind as if they were present.
*5: Nor could they (the Powers of Darkness) have more effectually prevented the progress of the Faith, than by desolating the New World; by burying nations alive in mines, or consigning them in all their errors to the sword. Relacion de B. de las Casas.
*6: Not man alone, but many other animals became extinct there.

CANTO XII

**A Vision**

Still would I speak of Him before I went,
Who among us a life of sorrow spent,
And, dying, left a world his monument;
Still, if the time allow'd! My Hour draws near;
But He will prompt me when I faint with fear.
Alas, He hears me not! He cannot hear!

Twice the Moon fill'd her silver urn with light.
Then from the Throne an Angel wing'd his flight;
He, who unfix'd the compass, and assign'd
O'er the wild waves a pathway to the wind;
Who, while approach'd by none but Spirits pure,
Wrought, in his progress thro' the dread obscure,
Signs like the ethereal bow, that shall endure! [*1]
Before the great Discoverer, laid to rest,
He stood, and thus his secret soul address'd.

"The wind recalls thee; its still voice obey.
Millions await thy coming; hence, away.
To thee blest tidings of great joy consign'd,
Another Nature, and a new Mankind!
The vain to dream, the wise to doubt shall cense;
Young men be glad, and old depart in peace!
Hence! tho' assembling in the fields of air,
Now, in a night of clouds, thy Foes prepare
To rock the globe with elemental wars,
And dash the floods of ocean to the stars; [*2]
To bid the meek repine, the valiant weep,
And Thee restore thy Secret to the Deep! [*3]
Not then to leave Thee! to their vengeance cast,
Thy heart their aliment, their dire repast!
To other eyes shall MEXICO unfold
Her feather'd tapestries, and roofs of gold.
To other eyes, from distant cliff descried,
Shall the PACIFIC roll his ample tide.
Chains thy reward! beyond the ATLANTIC wave
Hung in thy chamber, buried in thy grave!
Thy reverend form to time and grief a prey,
A phantom wandering in the light of day!
What tho' thy grey hairs to the dust descend,
Their scent shall track thee, track thee to the end;
Thy sons reproach'd with their great father's fame,
And on his world inscrib'd another's name!
That world a prison-house, full of sights of woe,
Where groans burst forth, and tears in torrents flow!
These gardens of the sun, sacred to song,
By dogs of carnage, howling loud and long, [*4]
Swept till the voyager, in the desert air,
Starts back to hear his alter'd accents there! [*5]
Not thine the olive, but the sword to bring,
Not peace, but war! Yet from these shores shall spring
Peace without end; [*6] from these, with blood defil'd,
Spread the pure spirit of thy Master mild!
Here, in His train, shall arts and arms attend,
Arts to adorn, and arms but to defend.
Assembling here, all nations shall be blest;
The sad be comforted; the weary rest:
Untouch'd shall drop the fetters from the slave;
And He shall rule the world he died to save!
Hence, and rejoice. The glorious work is done.
A spark is thrown that shall eclipse the sun!
And, tho' bad men shall long thy course pursue,
As erst the ravening brood o'er chaos flew,
He, whom I serve, shall vindicate his reign;
The spoiler spoil'd of all; the slayer slain; [*7]
The tyrant's self, oppressing and opprest,
Mid gems and gold unenvied and unblest: [*8]
While to the starry sphere thy name shall rise,

(Not there unsung thy generous enterprise!)
Thine in all hearts to dwell by Fame enshrin'd,
With those, the Few, that live but for Mankind."

*1: It is remarkable that these phenomena still remain among the mysteries of nature.
[*2: When he entered the Tagus, all the seamen ran from all parts to behold, as it were some
wonder, a ship that had escaped so terrible a storm. F. Columbus, c. 40.
*3: I wrote on a parchment that I had discovered what I had promised! and, having put it into a cask,
I threw it into the sea. Ibid. c. 37.
*4: One of these, on account of his extraordinary sagacity and fierceness, received the full allowance
of a soldier. His name was Bezerillo.
*5: No unusual effect of an exuberant vegetation. 'The air was so vitiated,' says an African traveller,
'that our torches burnt dim, and seemed ready to be extinguished; and even the human voice lost its
natural tone.'
*6: See Washington's farewell address to his fellow-citizens.
*7: Cortes, Pizarro. 'Almost all,' says Las Casas, 'have perished. The innocent blood, which they had
shed, cried aloud for vengeance; the sighs, the tears of so many victims went up before God.'
**: L'Espagne a fâit comme ce roi insensé qui demanda que tout ce qu'il toucheroit se convertit en or,
et qui fut obligé de revenir aux dieux pour les prier de finir sa misère. Montesquieu.

On the two last leaves, and written in another hand, are some stanzas in the romance or ballad
measure of the Spaniards. The subject is an adventure soon related.

Thy lonely watch-tower, Larenille,
Had lost the western sun;
And loud and long from hill to hill
Echoed the evening-gun,
When Hernan, rising on his oar,
Shot like an arrow from the shore.
"Those lights are on St. Mary's Isle;
They glimmer from the sacred pile." [*1]
The waves were rough; the hour was late.
But soon across the Tinto borne,
Thrice he blew the signal-horn,
He blew and would not wait.
Home by his dangerous path he went;
Leaving, in rich habiliment,
Two Strangers at the Convent-gate.

They ascended by steps hewn out in the rock; and, having asked for admittance, were lodged there,

Brothers in arms the Guests appear'd;
The Youngest with a Princely grace!
Short and sable was his beard,
Thoughtful and wan his face.
His velvet cap a medal bore,
And ermine fring'd his broider'd vest;
And, ever sparkling on his breast,
An image of St. John he wore. [*2]

The Eldest had a rougher aspect, and there was craft in his eye. He stood a little behind in a long black mantle, his hand resting upon the hilt of his sword; and his white hat and white shoes glittered in the moon-shine.

"Not here unwelcome, tho' unknown.
Enter and rest!" the Friar said.
The moon, that thro' the portal shone,
Shone on his reverend head.
Thro' many a court and gallery dim
Slowly he led, the burial-hymn
Swelling from the distant choir.
But now the holy men retire;
The arched cloisters issuing thro'
In long long order, two and two.

When other sounds had died away,
And the waves were heard alone,
They enter'd, tho' unus'd to pray,
Where God was worshipp'd, night and day,
And the dead knelt round in stone;
They enter'd, and from aisle to aisle
Wander'd with folded arms awhile,
Where on his altar-tomb reclin'd
The crosier'd Abbot; and the Knight
In harness for the Christian fight,
His hands in supplication join'd;
Then said as in a solemn mood,
"Now stand we where COLUMBUS stood!"

"PEREZ, [*3] thou good old man," they cried,
"And art thou in thy place of rest?
Tho' in the western world His grave, [*4]
That other world, the gift He gave, [*5]
Would ye were sleeping side by side!
Of all his friends He lov'd thee best."

The supper in the chamber done,
Much of a Southern Sea they spake,
And of that glorious City [*6] won
Near the setting of the Sun,
Thron'd in a silver lake;
Of seven kings in chains of gold [*7]
And deeds of death by tongue untold,
Deeds such as breath'd in secret there
Had shaken the Confession-chair!

The Eldest swore by our Lady, the Youngest by his conscience; while the Franciscan, sitting by in his grey habit, turned away and crossed himself again and again. "Here is a little book," said he at last, "the work of one in his shroud below. It tells of things you have mentioned; and, were Cortes and Pizarro here, it might perhaps make them reflect for a moment."

The Youngest smiled as he took it into his hand. He read it aloud to his companion with an unfaltering voice; but, when he laid it down, a silence ensued; nor was he seen to smile again that night. [*8] "The curse is heavy," said he at parting, "but Cortes may live to disappoint it." "Aye, and Pizarro too!"

*1: The Convent of Rábida.
*2: See Bernal Diaz, c. 203; and also a well-known portrait of Cortes, ascribed to Titian. Cortes was now in the 43d, Pizarro in the 60th year of his age.
*3: Late Superior of the House.
*4: In the chancel of the cathedral of St. Domingo.
*5: The words of the epitaph. "A Castilia y a Leon Nuevo Mundo dio Colon."
*6: Mexico.
*7: Afterwards the arms of Cortes and his descendants.
*8: 'After the death of Guatimotzin,' says B. Diaz, 'he became gloomy and restless; rising continually from his bed, and wandering about in the dark.'. 'Nothing prospered with him; and it was ascribed to the curses he was loaded with.'

A circumstance, recorded by Herrera, renders this visit not improbable. 'In May, 1528, Cortes arrived unexpectedly at Palos; and, soon after he had landed, he and Pizarro met and rejoiced; and it was remarkable that they should meet, as they were two of the most renowned men in the world.' B. Diaz makes no mention of the interview; but, relating an occurrence that took place at this time in Palos, says, 'that Cortes was now absent at Nuestra Senora de la Rábida.' The Convent is within half a league of the town.

www.ingramcontent.com/pod-product-compliance
Lightning Source LLC
Chambersburg PA
CBHW060050050426
42448CB00011B/2382